THE FO[UR]
MAGIC MOVES TO
WINNING GOLF

JOE DANTE

WITH LEN ELLIOTT

DRAWINGS BY WILLIAM CANFIELD

DOUBLEDAY

NEW YORK   LONDON   TORONTO   SYDNEY   AUCKLAND

A MAIN STREET BOOK

PUBLISHED BY DOUBLEDAY

a division of Bantam Doubleday Dell Publishing Group, Inc.

1540 Broadway, New York, New York 10036

MAIN STREET BOOKS and the portrayal of a building with a tree are
trademarks of Doubleday, a division of Bantam Doubleday Dell
Publishing Group, Inc.

Library of Congress Catalog Card Number: 61-17141

ISBN 0-385-47776-7

Contents

Introduction

This is a different kind of golf book. If it were not, there would be no excuse for our writing it, the publisher's printing it, or your reading it.

To say that it is *different* is a mild understatement. It is radical, heretical, iconoclastic. We expect that it will stir violent controversy.

The book is different for several reasons. First, we do not go along with those whose thought—though unspoken—is that most golfers are hopeless. We do not believe that a player who scores habitually around 94 or 98 or 110 should be left to freeze at whatever altitude he is struggling. That player, and any player, can be helped, and helped a great deal. We believe he can be taught to play a very respectable game. But he can be taught only by learning all over again how to swing the club. We believe that anybody in possession of all his physical members and mental faculties—barring only those who are too old, or too young, or too weak—can play much better golf than he plays now. And we will show you how it can be done.

In order to do this, we take a completely fresh approach—the second difference from other golf books. This is where the heretical and hence controversial aspect begins to show itself.

In thinking about the swing, in teaching the game, in experimenting over the years, and in reading and listening, we have come to the conclusion that a great deal of what is said and written about golf is wrong. A great mass of misinformation has accumulated. This we propose to sweep away. Many of the most revered, almost sacred, precepts, will be given some harsh treatment. A lot of them will be shown up as complete, though innocent, frauds. If good golf is to be learned and the poor player is to improve, a purging must take place, painful as it may be. Only in this way can the new swing, based on the proper principles and movements, be built.

Here, perhaps to soften the blow, it should be explained to the faithful how the false doctrines on which they have depended for so long, ever came to be established. The golf swing always has been an elusive, almost mysterious, thing. With no high-speed photography to aid them, no moving pictures, only the naked eye to tell them, the experts at the turn of the century had to do a lot of guessing, theorizing, and rationalizing. They ascribed reasons and causes for things because the reasons and causes *seemed* to fit. There was no microscope under which the swing could be placed and the theories proved or disproved.

All this led to a great, uncontrolled growth of ideas. Many of these, through long reiteration, came to be accepted as sound principles. Actually they were convenient conjectures, some of the rankest type, but for lack of proof to the contrary they have been looked upon as pearls of wisdom. They still spring out at us today, almost automatically, in such hackneyed exclamations as: "I looked up." "You quit on the shot." "Pull down with your left hand." These banalities have conditioned our thinking about golf until, truthfully, we have become lost in them.

Hence, much that we have learned must be forgotten, deliberately banished from our minds. Feelings that we have grown accustomed to must be extirpated. Actions that have become second nature to us must be somehow intercepted and prevented from taking place. In short, the board must be wiped clean.

Once that is done we will proceed to our third main theme: the elimination of errors.

Any football coach will tell you that football games are not won; they are lost by mistakes. The same concept can be applied to golf. Good scores are rarely the result of a succession of brilliant shots. They result from the absence of many bad shots. Conversely, the bad round of golf is the result of a lot of bad shots. In other words, what might have been a good round or a winning round, is lost by mistakes.

These mistakes can be of many kinds. Most of the top pro's mistakes come on or around the greens. He hits a short pitch or a chip that doesn't get close to the hole, or he misjudges the speed or roll of a green and takes a putt too many. These usually make the difference, for him, between a 71 and a 67.

But for the average golfer the mistakes that are most costly are bad shots off the tee and through the fairway. These get him into all kinds of trouble—into woods, traps, rough, brooks, ponds, out of bounds, and what have you.

These mistakes, in turn, stem from a swing that is basically bad. The bad swing, in its turn, is caused by a failure in execution *at one or more of four critical points*. Furthermore, golfers make the same mistakes at the same points, and this is true whether you test the point with two golfers or two thousand. Their mistakes can be broken down into the same basic wrong movements, occurring at the same critical places in the swing. This is one of the few definite, invariable patterns to be found in the bad golf swing.

These we have called the Four Fatal Flaws. Most poor or mediocre players manage to incorporate all four into one swing. Others have fewer, and score better. Our purpose is to expose these Four Fatal Flaws, examine them, explain them, eliminate them, and replace them with the right actions, which become the Four Magic Moves.

With the right moves instead of the wrong ones your swing will be better, your mistakes will be fewer, and your score will be lower.

Some of the Magic Moves will be new to you, and they will feel strange and awkward, as any new action does for a while. We can only insist that you follow our instructions to the letter, for we know that if you do the result will be very quickly apparent in the way the ball goes and the way you feel as you hit it.

During the explanation you will be given a picture and an understanding of the swing, particularly of the puzzling action of the club head, that will be entirely new. This is one of the most important parts of our book. It embodies a mechanical principle—the conservation of angular momentum—which has never before been explained in connection with the golf swing. This, indeed, borders on the magic. An understanding of this principle alone will make golf an easier game.

After dealing with the full swing we will go into a detailed description of the short game, including putting, the trouble shots, and, finally, the mental or thinking side of golf.

With this you will have acquired the knowledge and the weapons for a golf game far better than any you have known. It will then be up to you to use them.

1 *What You Can Do*

Yes, you can play better golf. Anyone can, once he gives himself a chance by learning what to do and how to do it. You who score over 100 can break 100. The 90 player can get into the 80's. The high 80's can drop to the low 80's. And the low-80 man can break the barrier into the 70's.

And don't tell us this is a gross exaggeration, already disproved by the frustrated millions who play this most fascinating of games. We assure you it is not an exaggeration. It has not been disproved. It is true.

We are not saying that all you have to do is read this book and go out the next afternoon and knock ten strokes off your score. What we are saying is that anybody who diligently applies himself to the principles laid down here, can cut a startling number of shots from his game.

The diligent application will involve several things. It will mean changing your mental attitude, for one. It will mean changing your swing. It will mean the determination to practice. And it will mean the time to play golf from two to as much as four times a week.

This price is not exorbitant. Sweat will be demanded, yes; but blood and tears are not involved. If you are willing to pay the price you can improve your game remarkably. You can play winning golf in your own handicap circle, and we don't care whether that circle is now around 82 or 112. You can drop to a faster circle. Depending on your present altitude, you can cut from five to fifteen strokes from your score.

You may have wondered, in a moment of idle reflection about this game, why more people don't play better golf than they do. It should be a simple game. You are hitting a ball that doesn't move. You are swinging clubs that have been designed with a great deal of care, involving time, money, and engineering skill. No one does anything to hinder you, either, or even to distract you.

One reason most of our scores stay high is our mental approach to the game. We are beaten before we start. The game has defeated the player for so many generations that the player now has an inferiority complex that would defy the combined skills of Freud, Jung, and Adler. To the man

7

who habitually goes around in 93, the thought of breaking into the 70's is the height of absurdity.

A complete reorientation is necessary. This has been accomplished in other sports, particularly in track and field. The four-minute mile, the seven-foot high jump, the sixty-foot shot-put are only three examples. It would take a superman, the track experts said, to run a mile in under four minutes. But once Dr. Roger Bannister did it a new plateau was established, onto which many other milers soon proceeded to climb. Back in 1920 Dick Landon won the Olympic high jump with 6 feet $4\frac{3}{4}$ inches. At Rome in 1960 a leap of 7 feet $\frac{1}{4}$ inch was good for only third place.

The point here is that mental barriers were broken, as well as those of time and altitude. The 96 golfer has a similar mental barrier, and it, too, must be shattered.

Naturally, Dr. Bannister and the other pioneers in the track and field record-breaking did not set their marks merely by thinking they could. The new marks stemmed from improved training methods and, especially in the field events, from vastly better techniques.

Here we come very close to golf. Golf is a game of techniques. Training, in the sense of physical conditioning, is relatively not of great importance, unless we are engaged in tournament play. The average man, once he gets out on the course a few times in the spring, finds no physical difficulty in playing an eighteen-hole round. Often he is fresh enough to play eighteen more holes, or nine, anyway.

But technique is something vastly different. A siege of training that would bring a man to peak physical condition probably would not knock one stroke off his score for eighteen holes. But a 50 per cent improvement in his technique of hitting the ball—his swing—could drop his score from the 90's into the 70's.

That technique is what we are looking for so desperately. Why don't we have it?

The answer, in the large general sense, is because the golf swing is extremely subtle. The essential actions are small actions, not readily seen with the naked eye, and from which attention is constantly diverted by the larger, more spectacular actions which surround them.

A second reason is that golf always has had the peculiar

faculty of making its players think they were doing things that they were not doing at all, and vice versa. This led, a long time ago, to the establishment of a great many theories and principles which seemed sound and reasonable but which were altogether wrong.

For example. Around the time of World War I the late Jim Dante, one of the authors of *The Nine Bad Shots of Golf,* was a young assistant pro at the Baltusrol Golf Club in Springfield, New Jersey. Harry Vardon, the great English professional, was touring America. He played a round at Baltusrol and explained his theories and his teaching methods to the Baltusrol pro, the late George Low. Low later passed them on to his assistants.

"But Mr. Low," objected the observant Dante, "Vardon doesn't hit the ball the way he says to hit it."

"The hell with how Vardon hits the ball!" roared Low. "You teach the way Vardon says, or look for another job."

Eventually the advent of slow-motion pictures showed that Dante was right. Vardon did not hit the ball as he said he did, which was as he *thought* he did. If the great Harry had ever swung at a ball with a throw of the club head from the top, as though to drive a stake into the ground (which was what he believed), he would never have won any tournament, much less six British Opens and one American.

This insidious incitement to self-delusion is without the slightest doubt one of the fundamental characteristics of golf. It accounts, perhaps more than any other one thing, for the painful slowness in the advancement of technique.

Just how slow this has been can be shown by one other example. Golf enjoyed wide popularity in Scotland as long ago as the middle of the fifteenth century. So many Scots were playing it that it interfered with the more important pursuit of archery, which was the means of national defense. In 1457, not long after the death of Joan of Arc and thirty-five years before Columbus sailed for the New World, the now famous edict of the Scottish parliament was issued which "decreted and ordained that wapinshawingis [passage or exhibition of arms] behalden by the lordis and baronis spirituale and temporale, four times in the zeir; and that the futeball and golf be utterly cryit doun, and nocht usit. . . ."

With all the golf being played then, it is inconceivable

that the Scots were not trying to figure out the best way to stand up to the ball, to grip the club, and to swing it.

Yet it was five hundred years later, in the middle of the twentieth century, before the teaching committee of the Professional Golfers' Association of America finally elicited enough agreement among its members to put in writing what it considered to be, and what it entitled: "The Five Basic Principles of the Swing."

Even allowing for the many and radical changes in balls and clubs, which have called for somewhat different methods over the centuries, it is still amazing that the basic principles of the swing escaped detection. But since they did, it is not amazing that so many widely differing theories have taken root and grown—to the eternal frustration of the average player.

This brings us back to our original thought: Why don't more people play better golf than they do?

The blunt truth is that they don't because the golf swing is heavily overlaid with a sludge of fallacy, misunderstanding, faulty theory, myth, and just plain ignorance. So thick is this coating that it is a wonder anyone ever gets through it and down to the hard, clean mechanics of the sound swing.

It is this sludge, most of which has been covering the swing for so long that it now acts as an insulation, that we will cut away in this book.

Once the myths and fallacies are exploded and the true machinery of the swing is laid bare for all to see and understand, golf becomes a much less difficult game.

2 Sweeping Out the Rubbish

The fallacies of golf are many and of various kinds. Some deal with the mental approach, some with a specific action, others with the mechanical principles which underlie the swing.

We will not attempt here to make a complete list. We will cover the two dozen or more that are most prevalent and have caused and still cause the most damage, and particularly those which must be exploded thoroughly if you are to assimilate the new thoughts, principles, and actions we will give you in this book.

Watch carefully. The fuse is lit!

"Relax." Rubbish. This fallacy is so old it should have been dead long ago. But it is a hardy perennial, and it has come down to us through generations of golf teachers right to the present day.

On the very face of it the advice is foolish. When you swing a golf club you are taking a comparatively violent action. Is there any other violent action you take while you are relaxed? Stop and think. Of course there isn't. It's impossible. Do Ben Hogan or Cary Middlecoff or Arnold Palmer look relaxed when they take their stance or hit those prodigious drives? If they are, why are their lips compressed and their features contorted, as countless pictures show they are?

It is easy to see how "Relax" became fixed in the language of the golf teacher. He gives lessons to a great number of middle-aged men and women who never in their lives have done anything of an athletic nature. When these people get on the lesson tee they are so self-conscious and frightened that they tense up to the point, almost, of absolute rigidity. In order for them to swing the club at all, the pro has to loosen them up to some extent. He tells them to relax. Then, since that advice has a beneficial effect, he promptly adopts an unsound line of thought. If a little is good, he thinks, a lot must be much better. He now makes a fetish of relaxation. Everybody has to relax as soon as he takes hold of a club.

11

We do not want a rigidity of the *rigor mortis* variety. But we do want a firmness, a feeling of muscular movement under constant control, ready for instant response.

Nor do we want a mental relaxation either. Don't get the idea your mind should be a complete blank when you step up to a shot. If it is, you might as well be asleep. The mind should be alert, thinking about what should be done and what should not be done, which side the trouble lies on, which way the wind is blowing, whether the tactical situation of the match or round calls for safety or boldness, and what adjustments, if any, should be made in the swing.

So forget everything you have heard about relaxing. For the purposes of playing good golf it is sheer rubbish.

"Use a light grip." This is a first cousin of "Relax." They go together, naturally. If you are completely relaxed as you address the ball, you are sure to have a light grip. One of our modern masters, Sam Snead, wants us to grip the club with no more pressure than we would use in handling a knife and fork. The immortal Bob Jones had a grip so light, in his heyday, that his left hand opened at the top of the swing, and he wanted it to open.

In the face of such advocates, we would certainly be the last to say that you can't play good golf with a light grip, but we do say, emphatically, that better and more consistent golf will be played by the average golfer when he adopts a tight grip. And by tight we mean tight all the way through, from address to the end of the follow-through.

It is noticeable that the top pros of the modern era are all firm-to-tight grippers, and that their hands (Snead's included) never loosen, even a little bit, at the top of the swing.

We do not mean that the grip should be so tight that it stiffens and cramps the muscles of the wrists and forearms. But, with practice, a surprisingly tight grip can be taken with the fingers and hands without stiffening the forearms. That is the grip we want. And it must be kept that way all through the swing.

"Be loose." This is the second cousin of "Relax." At first glance they may look like twins, but there is a difference.

Your swing can be loose even though you are not wholly relaxed. This becomes possible with a big hip turn on the backswing, a sway, bad wrist and foot action, and a certain type of grip.

Back in the 1920's and 1930's such a swing was thought to be highly desirable, and the fellow who had it was spoken of, admiringly, as being "loose as ashes."

Regardless of what the pros write or say, their swings in the 1950's were very definitely tight. They were shorter, more compact, with less movement of fewer parts. This tight swing was gradually developed by the American touring pros, whose very livelihood depended on how long and how straight they could hit the ball.

Tension, once thought to be the deadly enemy of good golf, now is rightly regarded as something to be striven for. A restricted turn of the hips on the backswing, along with a full turn of the shoulders, a different wrist action, and a tight grip all combine to produce the muscular tension that, when released, gives greater power to the swing.

When a swing is loose there are several parts of the body that are just going along for the ride, as it were; they contribute nothing. The pros today want no parts of the body to go into the action which are not working parts. And isn't this a sound principle?

"Take the club back inside." The idea here is based on producing the inside-out swing. The thought is that, if the club should approach the ball from the inside on the downswing, why not facilitate matters by taking the club back well on an inside line?

Going back sharply on the inside is something that is not taught, we are happy to say, by many pros. It is something that the average club player figures out for himself. He can't hit the ball with an inside-out swing, but he thinks he can do it by going back on the inside. So, in his efforts, and backed by a lot of misdirected determination, he comes back more and more to the inside, until he is almost whipping the club around his knees. Yet he still hits from the outside, and he can't understand it.

The fallacy in this is that the inside-out swing is not produced by the way the club is taken back, but by the way it is brought down. You can take the club back on the outside and still bring it down on the inside, hitting the ball with an inside-out swing.

"The club follows the same path coming down that it takes going up." The thinking here is closely allied to the last misconception. It is surprising how many people, who should know better, still think that the club head follows only a single path going up and coming down.

The club head does no such thing, in the correct swing. It comes down inside the path it took going up. This is accomplished not by any tricky hand action or even by conscious effort, but by the correct hip and (especially) shoulder actions at the beginning of the downswing. With these actions the club automatically shifts the swing plane to the inside. When these hip and shoulder actions are not correct, they shift the plane from the inside to the outside coming down.

But the conception of the club head following a single path is astonishingly common. We knew one intelligent young fellow—he hadn't yet played much golf—who carried this thought to a ridiculous extreme. His idea was that he would hit the ball straight if he kept the plane of the swing —both backward and forward—completely vertical. You have never seen, we assure you, such fantastic gyrations as this misdirected effort brought forth. You have never seen such an upright swing either. We mention this merely to show how far off base an intelligent but uninformed person can get when he starts to think about golf.

"Pause at the top." This has been a much-discussed action for a long time, some theorists favoring it and some condemning it. The general argument for it is that it gives the club a chance to change direction. It is an established mechanical principle that any object moving in one direction must come to a complete stop before moving in the opposite direction. This the club head certainly does, whether or not we see it or are conscious of it.

Thus far those who take this position are right. But what the average player thinks of when he thinks of a pause at the top, is that not only does the club stop for an instant, but that everything stops—shoulders, trunk, hips, knees. In effect, he freezes.

This is wrong. What happens at the top of the swing is that while the club is stationary for a fraction of a second before it changes direction, *the lower part of the body is moving*—moving into the downswing. This movement, actually, begins before the club gets all the way back. The pictures of any good golfer show this action and show it invariably. There can be no argument about it.

On the other hand, when a player freezes at the top he is almost certain to destroy whatever rhythm he had in his swing and to ruin the swing itself. Advocates of the pause claim it helps the player to start the downswing in a leisurely manner. Nonsense. To freeze at the top causes the average player to do just the opposite. He takes off like lightning on the downswing, because he has lost motion and rhythm and must then move from, as it were, a "standing start."

What about Middlecoff? you will ask. Doesn't he have a pronounced pause at the top? The answer is that Middlecoff's *club* is stationary at the top longer than the other top-flighters', but his knees and hips are moving. The latter you don't notice; you are looking only at his club. The thing that makes the Middlecoff pause so obvious is that while the doctor moves the lower part of his body as early as the other pros, his shoulders move a shade later, and as long as his shoulders don't move, the club doesn't move.

So forget about the pause at the top. If your swing is right you will get all the pause that is necessary, and without trying.

"Turn the hips to the left." This well-meant advice has spoiled more golf swings than all the caddies who ever rattled a bag of clubs.

What is meant here is that the first movement of the downswing should be a turning of the hips to the left. They are turned to the right as the body turns and coils to the right on the backswing, and as the weight goes over to the right leg. Therefore, you have been told, start the downswing by turning the hips to the left.

This instruction has caused its widespread damage because it has come from such high places. It is pronounced by no less an authority than Ben Hogan, who even writes of it as "spinning the hips."

But to turn the hips to the left as the first movement of the downswing is asking for disaster. Nothing less.

There is no telling how many home-club pros all over the world have had to put the brakes on hip-spinning among their members. The poor pupil, getting to the top of the swing, turns his hips violently to the left, leaves his weight on his right leg, brings the club down across the ball, hits a horrible shot, and then argues with the pro.

The turning of the hips does take place, of course. But they turn naturally, and they turn only after they have *first moved laterally to the left*. You will find, if you try to move your hips laterally as far as you can, that they will turn as they move toward the limit of extension. In fact, you can hardly stop them from turning.

If the lateral movement is not made, the weight will be very liable to stay over on the right leg instead of shifting to the left, as it must. If the weight doesn't move ahead of the swing, the shot will be ruined.

What actually takes place is a lateral turn of the hips.

It is quite possible that with some, as Hogan says, the lateral movement takes place involuntarily and that all they have to think about is the turning. This is undoubtedly true in his particular case and in those of a few others who keep a great deal of weight on the left leg during the backswing. But in the vast majority the reverse is true—the turn is involuntary but the lateral shift must be a conscious effort.

Another thought that may help you is that it is physically possible to turn the hips without moving them laterally, but it is almost impossible to move them to the limit laterally without turning them.

The importance of the lateral movement was stressed by Dow Finsterwald when we once asked him to name the first movement of the downswing.

"Why, a turn of the hips to the left," answered the former PGA champion.

"You mean," we said, "just a turn? Nothing else?"

"Well, no," he replied, "you have to move them to the left too. If you didn't, you'd leave too much of your weight on your right leg. You have to get the weight over."

The actual effort many players make to do nothing more than turn the hips brings about two actions that will ruin any swing. The turn, without the lateral movement, leaves the weight on the right leg, as we have seen, and it throws the arc of the swing outside the line of flight, so that the club head comes to the ball from the outside in, instead of from the inside out, as it must if a good shot is to be hit.

So don't think of turning your hips. Think of moving them laterally. It's a lateral turn, of which you will hear much more later.

"Keep the head still." This impossible advice has been given in one form or another for about as long as there has been any literature on golf: "Keep your head down." "Keep your head still." "Keep your head fixed." "Keep your eye on the ball." "Don't lift your head." "Don't look up." You've heard these directions a thousand times.

If they would only say, "Keep your head back," they would be much closer to being right. Because the head does have to stay back, whether or not it moves.

But the head does move. A careful study of pictures of the best golfers in the modern game reveals a very definite pattern of movement. The head stays steady on the back-swing, or perhaps turns on the neck a little to the right. Once the downswing gets well under way, though, the head moves to the right and comes down. It doesn't move ten or twelve inches, nothing like that. But it does move, consistently, in the right-and-downward pattern from one to three inches, perhaps more.

This movement is not an idiosyncrasy of certain individuals. In the correct swing it must take place, and the pictures show that it does. Arnold Palmer, Bill Casper, Middlecoff, Snead, Hogan, Finsterwald, Byron Nelson—they all have it.

It is caused by the rocking shoulder movement that takes place, a rocking that brings the left shoulder up and the right shoulder down, and by the bowing-out of the body toward the target as the weight is moved far over to the left. The rocking shoulder movement causes the head to move to the right, the bowing-out of the body brings the head down.

These actions of the head will be explained in greater detail later, as we get into the Four Magic Moves. Meanwhile, don't let anyone convince you that the head doesn't move in a good golf swing. It has to.

"Start down with a pull of the left arm." If you've ever read any golf instruction you're pretty sure to have read this. Forget it. Starting the downswing by pulling down with the left arm can ruin your swing just as effectively as spinning your hips.

The pull-down technique, if such it can be called, is virtually certain to throw the swing outside as well as start it down too soon from the top. It also starts the downswing in the wrong place and with the wrong part of the body. The first move from the top is by the hips, which are close to the axis of the turning body. Any early action from the top by the arms is sure to bring about two other unwanted results—an early hit instead of a late one and an immediate loosening of the tension that has been built up during the backswing and which we want to hold as long as possible.

This pull-down idea has been repeated so often by so many top players in their writings that we feel they have come to believe they actually do start the downswing this way. What happens, we think, is that the top player is coiled so tight at the top that when he makes his hip movement to start down, it exerts a pull (which he feels) on his left arm, and he thus can easily believe it is the left-arm pull, rather than the hip, which starts everything. Certainly no pro is going to advocate any movement which he knows is wrong. The mistake is an honest one, but it is still a mistake.

We are also certain that some of the top-name players believe the arm pull is the thing to teach, whether they believe in it or not.

One of the best of the women pros was holding a clinic at a club a few years ago, and she was telling the girls to start down with a pull of the left arm. Afterward we were talking to her about the swing.

"Do you, yourself," we asked, "start down with a pull of your left arm?"

"No," she answered.

"Well, do you start with a pull of your right arm or right hand?"

"No," she replied. "In fact, I don't start down by pulling

anything."

The left-arm pull-down just seems to be something that
many pros feel ought to be said.

"Have the face open at the top." The old-timers make a
fetish of this position. The early pros who came to this country from Scotland and England were open-face swingers,
which means merely that at the top of the swing the face of
the club is vertical with the ground and the toe of the club
points directly down at the ground. This was the classic
method during the early years of golf in this country. So
strongly was it stressed that there are still today pros who
teach it and pupils who feel that the toe of the club should
point down.

The theory was that the open face would work to prevent a
hook and that the face would be closed or squared as it came
into the ball either by the body action or by rolling the
wrists into the shot. We have read it both ways and it certainly is a fact that the old pros taught a rolling wrist action.
They rolled to the right on the backswing, which was called
supination, and rolled to the left as they came through the
ball, which was known as pronation. Books have been written
on pronation.

Certainly the ball can be hit this way, and was by a great
many immortal players. But it's the hard way to do it. The
easy way, the modern way, will be described in a subsequent
chapter.

"Don't let the body or hands get ahead of the club." You
rarely hear this advice any more, but just in case you have
and it's sticking in the back of your head somewhere, forget
it.

What it meant was that the body, the hands, and the club
should all go through the ball together. Once slow-motion
pictures of the swing began to gain circulation it was seen,
of course, that the body always was ahead of the club, way
ahead of it, on the downswing, and that the hands led the
club all the way down, with the club barely catching up at
the ball.

"Be comfortable." Ah, yes, by all means be comfortable—
and play bad golf. If you are learning the game or if you

play it fairly well but want to improve, forget any idea of being comfortable. The golf swing feels comfortable and easy and simple to the expert, but only because he has swung the club so much.

The fact is, the swing, especially at the top, calls for a strained and certainly not comfortable position. You are deliberately turning and winding yourself up on your backswing and trying to attain a stretched, tension-filled position of the body. This isn't and cannot be, in the accepted sense, comfortable. As a matter of fact, the unconscious action of millions of pupils as they near the top of the swing is a movement that enables them to be comfortable. This movement, which is a bending of the left elbow and a cocking-back of the left wrist, enables them to get the club up and and back—even to overswing it—without being uncomfortable. This movement has to be fought against. So don't try to be comfortable. For the average golfer, the correct swing should be uncomfortable.

"Break the wrists late." One more sacred tenet bites the dust. Since the beginning of golfing time, almost, we have been admonished to break the wrists late on the backswing. This enables us to take the club back low to the ground and get a big arc. There is no gainsaying the fact that thousands of great golfers have done exactly this.

We do say, however, that it is not at all necessary and, further, that it does more harm than good.

There is no particular value in taking the club back low to the ground, except that it helps transfer the weight to the right leg. It isn't necessary for the transfer, though. So far as getting a big arc is concerned, that is strictly a fallacy. The length of the left arm determines the arc of the swing —the longer the arm the bigger the arc. The arc the club head follows is something else and something that is mistakenly regarded as important. Why should it be? The arc of the club head is decidedly smaller on the downswing than it is on a conventional backswing. We don't try for a big arc on the downswing; in fact, we try to have it as small as possible. So what is the value of a big arc on the backswing? You tell us.

The late wrist break also leads invariably to an open face at the top of the swing, which is something modern golfers have proved to be not only undesirable but dangerous. Since the pros have been moving toward a square or even somewhat closed face at the top, they have been breaking earlier. For the swing we will teach in this book, a late break is poison. If you have one, prepare to get rid of it.

"Swing the club head." Here is one of the most plausible principles golf teachers have ever come up with. Because it is so plausible, it is one of the most dangerous and misleading.

How can it possibly be wrong? you ask. We hit the ball with the club head, don't we? We have to get it to the ball. What do we do with it if we don't swing it?

As a quick explanation of what to do, we will say this: Swing your hands, not the club head.

Actually, that is the conclusion we reach in our exploration of this fallacy. Let's start at the beginning and put the horse in front of the cart, where he belongs.

Certainly we hit the ball with the club head, and of course the club head swings to get to the ball. But where do most of our troubles in golf originate? From efforts to manipulate, to do something with, the head of the club. We know we are going to hit the ball with it and we know the club head has to move rapidly to drive the ball very far. So immediately, from the top of the backswing, we try to move the club head. Our thoughts are on the club head, our efforts are centered on the club head.

The result is that we get the club head moving too fast too early. It gets ahead, relatively, of the unwinding body. It gets outside the proper plane. The wrist cock is used up early. So we hit, time after time, too soon and from the outside in. All because we are trying to do something *with the club head.*

That is the natural tendency in hitting a golf ball. Thinking of the club head and trying to manipulate it are instinctive actions. Now, if we are taught that the secret of golf is to "swing the club head," our instincts are not only encouraged but reinforced.

What we have to realize is that the head of the club is only a tool, and it does something to something else as we direct it. But this direction comes from our bodies and our hands, and those are the things we must think of. When you are driving an automobile and you turn a corner, you do not think of the front wheels of the car. You are conscious only of the pressure your hands exert on the steering wheel to guide the car where you want it to go, and of the movement of your feet to give it the necessary power.

If we do with our bodies and our hands what we should do with them, the head of the club will take care of itself. We don't have to think of it at all.

This is going to be very hard for most of you to get into your heads. But make up your minds to get it in, if you hope to improve your golf.

Where, you probably will demand, is the power to come from that makes the club head go fast at impact if we do not deliberately apply it?

The power, briefly, comes from the action of the body, supplemented in the later stages of the downswing by an effort to speed up the hands. This effort, however, must not be confused with an effort to speed up the club head. It is merely an attempt to make the hands travel faster along the arc they follow as they come down past the position of the ball. *The club head will take care of itself.*

This, as we said, is a rather brief explanation of why you should not try to swing the club head or even think of it. Our reasons will be further substantiated on later pages, when we get into the mechanical principles that govern the swing.

Meanwhile, forget about swinging the club head or doing anything else with it. We will show you later that this eternal preoccupation with the club head is one of the worst sins of golf.

"Hit against a firm left side." To anyone who ever has given much thought to the swing, this always has been something of a puzzle. We have been told on the one hand to hit against a firm left side and, on the other hand, to turn the hips and get the left hip out of the way so it won't block the swing. Can both instructions be right? Obviously not.

The image conveyed by the advice to hit against a firm left side is of the player stopping the unwinding of his body after he starts the downswing, holding the left side rigid, and then somehow hitting past it. This can be done, we admit, but no good shot could ever come out of it. Whether this is exactly what is meant by those recommending it, we cannot say, for they never have been able to explain to us just what they do mean.

Hitting against a firm left side is a myth. No good golfer ever does it. Pictures, both motion and sequence, show the left side moving steadily to the left on the downswing and then turning away from the direction line of the shot. The left side, in practically all good swings, bows out toward the target before the club reaches and passes the ball. With some players, former Open champion Dick Mayer for instance, this bowing-out is extremely pronounced. It is in Middlecoff too, and Hogan, Snead, Palmer, and Casper all show it.

What happens, of course, is that the left side, in a good swing, starts and stays far ahead of the club. It is always pulling and stretching. Hence there is always a feeling of great tension in it. It is this feeling, without a doubt, that long ago gave rise to the belief that we must keep the left side firm and hit against it.

Actually the left side is automatically kept taut and stretched in the correct swing, but it is moved far out of the way of the downswinging arms. These arms and hands do not hit "against" that left side. The left side gets out of their way, so they can hit through toward the target. And only by getting the left side out of the way can the full, free speed of the club ever be developed.

So throw out one more old piece of trash, one of the many that have doubtless kept you from realizing the potential you have as a golfer.

"Snap your wrists into the shot." The carnage this clinker has caused over the generations is staggering.

There is probably not one golfer who has not been urged, at some stage in his struggles, to snap his wrists. It is always well-meant advice, of course. The giver thinks he is being helpful. The recipient dutifully tries—and tries and tries. But the wrists won't snap.

The advice is sheer drivel.

In exploding this little number we will first define what is meant by snapping the wrists. To the golfer it means a very quick forward motion of the hands, hinging at the wrist joints, just before the club head strikes the ball. The hands are used much as we might use them in snapping a whip.

It is generally felt that the good golfers use this snapping action to whip the head of the club into the ball at greater speed. If the good golfers do it, why shouldn't the poor ones? As a consequence, the effort to put the snap into practice results in the player trying to move the head of the club with extra effort. It is something like what happens when we try to swing the club head, only now we are trying to snap it. All this results in is an even earlier expendage of the wrist cock, an earlier loss of power, a quicker hit, usually from the outside, and a worse shot. Again it is the preoccupation with the club head that is the root of the trouble. We are trying, by snapping the wrists, to snap the club head.

In reality a snapping action of a sort does take place in the good swing, but it takes place as the result of a mechanical principle, *not through any effort on the part of the player*.

Halfway down, in a good swing, the angle formed by the club and the left arm is still about what it was at the top. It is approximately a right angle. As the hands get nearer the ball the speed of the club increases and the angle begins to open up. As the hands reach the ball the head of the club is traveling much, much faster and the angle is almost 180 degrees. At a point about eighteen inches to two feet past the position of the ball (which is now in flight), the club head passes the hands and causes the right hand to climb over the left.

The climbing-over is a rather violent action, and it is definitely felt in the wrists. The later the hit, the sharper it is, too. So fast is the sequence of events, however, that the climbing-over action *seems* to take place before the ball is hit, and it *feels* as if the wrists were being snapped.

This feeling is one of the reasons, we are certain, for the prolonged popularity of the unfortunate advice. Coupled with it is the fact that for a long, long time it was believed we had to pronate. This was a deliberate turning-over of the wrists as they came into the ball. With this action the old-timers were positive they were snapping their wrists.

It is just one more example of the golfer's self-delusion.

Any reader can almost prove the foregoing explanation by taking a practice swing. With no ball to bother with, hold the wrist cock as long as you can but make no effort to snap your wrists. If your swing is anywhere nearly correct you will feel the fast climb-over action.

For complete proof, though, there is nothing to approach the sequence pictures of a seven-year-old child's swing, shown in Photo G. The catching-up action is shown clearly. This child, you may be dead sure, was never told to snap his wrists, and he couldn't have snapped them anyway.

So, into the ash can goes another misconception. If you will just swing the club right, the "wrist snap" will take care of itself.

"Hit hard with the right hand." The trouble with advice like this is that, while it is partly right, it can do more harm than good.

What is meant is to hit hard with the right hand in the low hitting area, just before impact. But we should hit just as hard with our left hand as with our right. And we do not mean hitting so that our hands bend to the left and get ahead of our wrists and forearms, either. That is disastrous. Hitting, to us, means moving the hands through the hitting area as fast as we can but with the wrists slightly ahead of the hands. No snapping action.

Another danger in even mentioning the right hand at the expense of the left, is that the right hand is usually our more active, responsive, and stronger hand for the reason that we are right-handed. The whole tendency in golf is for the right hand to take charge of the swing and overpower the left. This leads to hitting too soon and hitting from the outside, things the struggling club pro has been trying for years to stop his pupils from doing.

So, let's drop the right hand out of our thinking, so far as hitting the ball goes, anyway.

"Don't drop the right shoulder." You've been given this advice when you were in a fit of hitting the ground behind the ball—sclaffing, to give it the old Scottish name.

You've studied pictures of a good pro hitting the ball. Did

you ever see one in which the pro's right shoulder wasn't lower than his left?

Of course the right shoulder drops. It has to. It's lower than the left shoulder at the address and it's still lower at impact. The reason the pro hits the ball and not the ground is because he shifts his weight to the left, something you neglect to do when you are sclaffing.

Of course you should make no *effort* to drop the right shoulder. If the start down from the top is made correctly, the shoulder will come down naturally, and if the same move from the top is done right, the weight will shift to the left. You, too, will hit the ball and not the ground.

"Hit down on the ball." The topper is the one who gets this advice thrown at him.

No special effort, we can assure you, is necessary to hit down on the ball. We will hit down naturally, if our swing is right. There is no other way to hit.

But when the poor player, with the bad swing, is told to hit down on the ball, he starts to chop at it. He brings the club up quickly with more of a lift than a swing, then chops down, often with a bend of the right knee, so he'll be sure he is low enough. This violates all the principles of the swing, of course, and while the fellow may not top the ball he will quickly get himself into other troubles equally bad or worse.

"Use your natural swing." This advice is the ace of absurdities, for the very simple reason that the good golf swing is not a natural swing. It's an action that has to be learned. Not one adult in a million, who has never played golf, will step up to a ball and hit it with a good swing. He'll hit it with what, for him, is his natural swing, but it will be terrible.

It might be good advice to give a person who learned the game as a child, who has been working at it for years, and who is now trying to copy some other player's swing.

But the natural swing of the average adult is the one you see on driving ranges, public courses, and even on private courses, where a surprising number of members will brag about the fact that they never took a lesson. If you want the swing you laugh at in these places, then by all means use your own natural talents and hack away.

"Follow through." This one, thank heaven, is on the way out. The more intelligent teachers and players discovered quite some years ago that the follow-through was not the *cause* of a good shot, it was the *result*. But we are including it here because the advice still pops up often enough to be dangerous.

From the early days of golf in this country and for a long time afterward, the core of all instruction could be summed up in one sentence: "Head down, slow back, and follow through."

Whatever value the first two admonitions had was lost by the third. People tried to get good follow-throughs without ever realizing that they first had to have a reasonably good swing. Nobody yet has hit the ball with his follow-through, but an awful lot have tried to.

Once you have a good swing, which comes from the inside with a late hit instead of an early one, the speed of the club head will pull it up into the follow-through without any effort on your part. In fact, you can't stop it.

"Don't quit on the shot." Nothing quite matches this advice for its ability to infuriate. The poor player is having all kinds of trouble. He is hitting the ball as hard as he can with the swing he has. And then some member of the foursome, trying to be helpful, says: "You quit on the shot."

If the recipient of the advice isn't seized with apoplexy on the spot, it's because he doesn't know any more about the swing than the fellow who gave the advice. He thinks that, yes, he must have quit. And he tries to swing harder the next time.

The implication of the phrase is that somewhere during the downswing the player stopped trying and just let the swing finish itself. This is about as far wrong as it could be. The good player will occasionally do this—fail to hit hard through the ball—when he feels at the last moment that he has too much club, or a following breeze has sprung up, or something else. It is known as "coming off the shot." But the average player? No. His so-called quitting is not quitting at all. It is the result of a bad swing, and he will still "quit" even though he swings himself off his feet in an effort to hit hard.

The cause of what is called "quitting on the shot" is hitting too soon. The angle between the left arm and the club opens up early as the club starts down, instead of being retained. Thus the power that is gained by the late hit is expended much too early. With the wrist cock gone, there is little left to hit with. No matter how hard the player tries, he cannot produce anything more than a weak, flabby-looking slap at the ball. And the other players nod their heads sagely and think to themselves, if they don't come out and say it, "He quit on the shot."

This is one of the greatest misconceptions in golf and one of the commonest.

It is closely allied, of course, with a complete misunderstanding of how the wrist cock is retained through the first part of the downswing, and thus of how the late hit is accomplished. We have all seen pictures of the good player which show his hands entering the so-called hitting area. The hands are maybe a foot from being directly opposite the ball, but his wrist cock has been largely retained and the club head is a long way from the ball, still above the player's waist.

There is a widely held conviction that the only way the club head can be made to catch up with the hands in time to hit the ball, is through the player's own physical efforts. He must drive the club head through with his hands and wrists at the last instant. This is where the "wrist snap" comes in. Only a player of long experience and considerable strength, it is thought, can accomplish this.

A book appeared in the late 1950's, written by Dai Rees, then captain of the British Ryder Cup team. One part of it dealt with the late hit versus the early hit. It was Rees's opinion that only a young, strong professional should attempt to get the late hit; all others should be satisfied with the early hit. The others should be satisfied, in other words, to spend their golfing lives hitting too soon, hitting from the top.

This is nonsense. The late hit can be accomplished by a seven-year-old child. It is governed entirely by the early movement of the downswing, not by any action near the ball. If that first movement is correct, the hit will be late; if it is wrong, the hit will be early.

If this first movement from the top conforms to the mechanical principle that controls the action of the club head (which we will presently describe in full detail), then the wrist cock will be retained, the hit will be late, and the speed of the club head at impact will be high.

"Pronate your wrists." This one is very nearly dead, but we are including it so we can give it a final kick and send it, we hope, to its grave.

Pronation was the name given by the old pros to rolling the wrists into the shot at impact with the ball. The idea was that on the backswing the wrists were rolled to the right, opening the club face, and then rolled back to the left on the downswing to close it, or bring it square to the ball.

It was also generally accepted that pronation not only squared the face of the club but also added distance to the shot because the club head was turning over toward the ball at impact.

Most of the great golfers in the early years of the century used this action, many of them superlatively well. But it is worth noting that none of those players, Vardon included, were as consistent in their scoring as the top pros of today. The pronating of the wrists had to be timed to a nicety, obviously, if the ball were to be struck squarely. A little too much rolling, or too early, brought a hook or a smother; not enough left the face open and produced a slice. The best that can be said for pronation is that it is a great way to live dangerously.

"Pivot the body." There is nothing wrong with the pivot, except the connotation the word has and the way the action has been so often described. The pivot in golf means the turning and winding up of the body on the backswing. It is described as being made around a fixed axis. Diagrams have been printed showing the poor golfer pivoting around a long iron stake which passes through his head, body, right leg, and into the ground. Such an axis is as immovable as anyone could imagine. We also have been advised to make the turn as though we were standing in a barrel.

Both images are wrong, because the axis of the turn is not stationary. It moves. As the turn begins, the weight moves to the right leg, not all of it but a considerable part of it. This means the hips, which are the center of gravity, also move. It doesn't mean that we sway when the weight goes over, because our head and the upper part of our body stay in the same position. The iron stake, to carry out that analogy, could not be iron but something flexible which would bend in the middle.

The trouble with the word *pivot* is that we picture it as a turn around a fixed axis, and when we make it, we don't move the weight. We are very much inclined to leave the weight—too much of it at least—on the left leg. And when we do that we are in trouble. So, when you think of winding up the body, think of it as making a lateral turn with the weight moving.

"Positions at address and impact must be the same." More nonsense. About the only similarity between the positions is that the player is standing on both feet in each one. All you have to do to realize the differences is to think about them for a few seconds.

For instance, at address the position is stationary, the weight is about equally divided between the feet, both feet are flat on the ground, the hips are parallel to the direction line, the hands are even with the ball and the right shoulder is slightly lower than the left. But look at the position at impact. Here nearly every part of the body except the head is in violent movement. The weight is probably 80 per cent on the left foot. The left foot is flat but the right heel is off the ground and the foot is rolling in on the inside. The hips have moved and turned well past a position parallel to the direction line. The right shoulder is much lower than the left, which is higher than it was at address anyway. And the hands are slightly past the ball.

Why anyone should say these two positions are the same, or should be the same, is beyond us.

We have now examined and disposed of much of the advice that has obscured the golf swing with myth and ignorance far too long. We hope your mind has now been pretty well cleared of a lot of accumulated rubbish. It must be if you are to absorb and apply the fresh ideas to be given hereafter. Some of your most cherished convictions have probably been dealt with rather harshly in this first section. Maybe some of the excisions were painful. All we can say to reassure you is that an operation for appendicitis hurts too, but when the operation is necessary, you are better off without the appendix.

1 2 3

4 5 6

7 8

Photo G. Conservation of Angular Momentum operating in the swing of Joe Dante's seven-year-old son, Ross. The youngster brings the club down nicely, with the wrist cock well retained, in Nos. 1-5. In 6 he has reached the hitting position. In 7 his hands are slowing down slightly, though he doesn't realize it, and the club, with momentum flowing into it, is catching up. In 8 it has caught up and dispatched the ball.

31

3 Getting Set:
The Grip and the Stance

There can be no doubt whatever that the first mistakes a golfer can make are to hold the club with a defective grip and to stand up to the ball the wrong way. Either puts a heavy impost on a player before he makes a move to swing the club. Together they make a good shot almost impossible.

Any shot, of course, is measured by two standards. One is direction, the other is distance. Direction is governed partly by the position of the club face at impact and partly by the path the club head is following. Distance, on the other hand, is the product of club-head speed and the accuracy with which the head makes contact with the ball. These, in turn, are produced by body, arm, and hand action during the swing.

But the position of the club face is largely determined by the grip, and the path of the club head is influenced considerably by the stance. The grip, to a very large degree, determines whether the face will be square to the direction line, open, closed, or even hooded, therefore whether the ball flies straight, is sliced, hooked, smothered, or even skied. Any one of these shots brings trouble, and with trouble the strokes begin to mount up.

That is why the pros will tell you that the grip is the most important single factor in the game. Gene Sarazen has said the grip is 75 per cent of golf. To him and the other pros it is, because they have all the distance they need. They make the moves that bring distance—make them automatically, and have made them since they were kids. A change of a couple of millimeters in the placing of one hand on the grip, however, producing better direction, could make, for them, the difference between a 69 and a 65.

People do all kinds of peculiar things with both the grip and the stance, even to the extent of changing both after they have been taken. You've often seen a player stand up to the ball with both a stance and grip that were good, and then start to fiddle around. He changes his hands a little, then moves his feet a little. Then moves his hands another little bit, then shifts his feet again. By this time the grip no longer is a good one and neither is the stance. We once had a pupil who was a pretty good player and who learned easily; he had a peculiarly good faculty of doing just what he was told to do, without arguing about it. It was no trick for him to take a good grip and stand up to the ball perfectly. The trick was to make him hit the ball before he changed either of them.

Common Faults

The most common faults in the grip are holding the club entirely in the fingers of the left hand, placing the left hand too much on top of the shaft, and getting the right hand under the shaft.

An all-finger grip and getting the left hand on top, so that four knuckles show, go together. It's almost impossible to hold the club entirely in the fingers of the left, without getting the left on top of the shaft. Try it yourself and see.

The reason most people keep dropping the right hand lower and lower until it gets practically under the shaft, is that they feel they will get more power that way.

Well, they are all wrong and they go a long way toward ruining what might be a good shot. When the club is held entirely in the fingers of the left hand and that hand is on top of the shaft with three or four knuckles showing, there is an overpowering tendency to roll that hand over to the left as the club comes into the ball at impact. When this happens, of course, the face of the club is turned over and closed, or even hooded. The result is a bad smother or hook. That is what happens with some players.

The all-finger, left-hand-on-top position leads to another fault. It has a strong tendency to make the player bend the left hand back at the top of the swing and get the left wrist under the shaft. This opens the face at the top, and it must then be closed on the downswing. With the body and shoulder action most players have, plus their fear of getting the face closed too much, this is seldom accomplished. Hence we have what is by far the most common and exasperating bad shot of them all—the slice.

Another move is for the player to try to hold the face of

the club from turning as it goes through the ball. Then you see the lifting, lofting action which is so common, with the player trying to hold the face square long after it has hit the ball. This is a good way to bring on a slice.

When the right hand is dropped low, the faults of the left are compounded, for a low right hand tends to roll over at impact. The poor player may switch from slicing to smothering and go for several holes without getting the ball more than a few feet off the ground. This, we need hardly remind you, is a horrible experience.

Things go from bad to worse until the only thing certain is that the player will not hit two shots in a row in the same direction. He is all over the course, hacking out of trouble first on one side and then on the other.

On any course and in almost any foursome you will see many peculiar stances. Most of them are not fundamentally bad, except for one thing: standing with an "open" body. This means, simply, that although the feet are in a perfectly square position (an equal distance from the direction line), the hips and the shoulders are facing a little to the left.

These players are, in effect, aiming to the left of their target without realizing it.

You need hardly be reminded of the damage this can do. The player develops a pull to his shots, the ball starting out a shade to the left and, if it doesn't slice, staying to the left. There are usually just as much rough and as many traps to the left of a fairway or green as there are to the right, and the chronic puller is sure to find most of them.

There are other bad positions, such as bending over too much, standing too far from the ball, having the weight too far forward, and so on, but the "open" body is by all odds the most common fault the average player has in the stance department.

Let us turn now to the positive side and take the positions that will help so much to give us a square face at impact, a straight ball that goes where we aim it, and fewer shots.

Actually there is nothing mysterious about the grip. We merely want the club held in a certain way, a way that will help bring it to the top in the position we want and which will help bring it back to the ball at the correct angle to the line of flight.

Placing the Hands

Such a grip calls for the hands to be in practically direct opposition as they grasp the club—that is, with the palms facing each other squarely. The left hand is placed against the shaft in such a manner that the shaft makes a diagonal contact from the crook of the index finger across the palm. It is, with this left hand, a combination palm and finger grip. When this hand is closed the club should be held in the first two fingers and the palm. There should be a fold of flesh between the club and the little finger. This, as a matter of fact, is a check point by which you can tell whether you have the palm-and-finger grip.

Now we also want—nay, demand—that only two knuckles of this left hand be visible when the hand is closed tightly on the club. As you address the ball and look down at your hands, you must see no more than two knuckles, those at the base of the index finger and the big finger. Not four knuckles, not three knuckles, not one knuckle. Two knuckles! This is your second and last check point for the position of this hand (Figs. 1 and 2).

So much emphasis has been put on the left hand over the years that many people believe the right doesn't amount to much in the grip. They couldn't be more wrong. The right

Fig. 1. How the left hand should look on the club. The back of the hand is facing left, not up, two knuckles are visible, the thumb lies a little to the player's right on the shaft, and the V, between thumb and forefinger, points slightly to the player's right.

hand is very important, both in the way it grasps the club and in the way it fits against the left. Let's take the club first.

Fig. 2. Inside the left hand. The important point here is that the club lies diagonally across the palm, from the crook of the index finger, and comes out halfway between the root of the little finger and the base of the palm. There must always be a fold of flesh between the club and the root of the little finger.

It has been said that the grip with the right hand is a finger grip. This is true. But *where* in the fingers? There is only one place that is correct, and that is at the very base or root of the second and third fingers, where they meet the palm. This is the best place because there the club can be held most securely. There is not only less chance but less inclination, with such a grip, to loosen the hand at the top of the swing or anywhere else. Such a grip, because it is at the very edge of the palm, makes for a tighter connecting joint between arm and club, with less give than any other. It transmits more power when the ball is struck (Fig. 3).

Any grip higher in the fingers of the right hand, say along the inside of the middle knuckles of the second and third fingers, is untrustworthy. It is a loose grip to begin with, and the tendency is to loosen it further at the top of the swing. Finally, there is more give in it when the ball is hit.

We have identified the right-hand grip as being taken with the second and third fingers because, of course, the index finger is separated slightly from the middle finger and is hooked low around the club. The little finger, in the over-

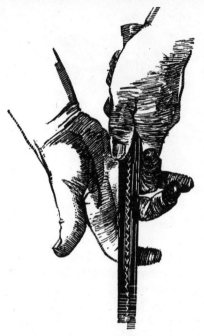

Fig. 3. How the right hand goes on. Here the club lies definitely in the fingers, but at the very roots of the second and third digits, with the forefinger getting ready to hook low around the shaft.

lapping or interlocking grips, does not touch the club at all. In the so-called ten-finger grip, though, the little finger would grasp the club exactly as the second and third do.

In taking our grip we recommend placing the left hand on the club first in its proper position, then sliding the right under the shaft, fingers extended and palm up. As the club slips into the little groove where the fingers meet the palm, slide no farther. Close the hand then, moving it up the shaft slightly so that the third finger fits against the index finger of the left hand and the little finger overlaps or lies on top of the left index finger.

You will find that the palm of the right comes up and faces directly to the left, and that the center of the base of the right hand fits snugly over the big knuckle at the base of the left thumb. Both thumbs will be on the shaft, the left lying a little to the right of the top (at about 2 o'clock in aviation parlance) and the right lying to the left of the top, at about 10 or 10:30 o'clock. The well-known V's,

Fig. 4. The right hand fitting against the left, with the center of the base of the right palm moving onto the big knuckle at the base of the left thumb.

formed by the folds of flesh between the thumb and fore-finger of each hand, should both point a shade to the right of the chin, to about the inside joint of the collar bone (Fig. 5).

Incidentally, one of the club manufacturers has a small ridge-line running down the underside of all its grips. This fits perfectly into the groove at the base of the fingers of the right hand, and practically locks the player into the correct right-hand position.

Ridge-line or not, however, this is the overlapping grip we

Fig. 5. The completed grip. Here we see the two knuckles of the left hand and the strong right hand, with the forefinger hooked low around the shaft, and the V's pointing somewhat to the player's right. The right-hand V always will point more to the right than that of the left because of the position of the club at the roots of the fingers.

must have. Its principal points are that the hands are opposed, the left has a palm-and-finger contact, the right a
finger grip alone—and that only two knuckles of the left are
visible at address.

Two slight refinements should be mentioned. The crook
of the right index finger, when the grip is completed, must
always be farther down the shaft than the end of the right
thumb. The crook of this index finger may be regarded, almost, as a hook, and it must never be higher than the tip

Fig. 6. The completed grip with the
club held up, showing how the little
finger of the right hand overlaps the
index finger of the left.

of the thumb. It is also permissible to place the overlapping
little finger down against the seam between the left hand's
index and big fingers. This is not too important. It may
feel more comfortable that way to some and it may give
a feeling of greater security to others. If you like the little
finger down in the seam instead of riding on top of the index
finger, by all means put it there.

We believe this grip is better than the interlocking or
the ten-finger grips. The pure baseball grip is not even to
be considered; it has nothing whatever to recommend it.

The overlapping grip gives us a better chance to maintain full and tight contact with both hands at all stages of
the swing. And this we must have.

Hold It Tight

The next question is how tight to take this grip. Let it be

known here and now that we do not go along with the knife-and-fork school of gripping—unless it should be a very dull knife operating on a tough piece of meat. In other words, we do not want a loose grip. Not even a firm grip. We want a tight grip.

We do not mean so tight that the muscles of the upper arms and shoulders are tied up with tension. By no means. But we do want those hands tight on the club. What, you will ask, about the wrists? If they are tight, won't the swing be stiff and wooden? And how will I get my wrist break?

Never mind about the wrists. We have rarely seen anybody too stiff or too tight in swinging a golf club (except perhaps for frightened beginners), but we have seen thousands too loose. The whole tendency in pupils is to take too light a grip. The loose grip leads into faults—opening the hands at the top, collapsing the left wrist, overswinging, and so on. The tight grip, though it may feel awkward for a while, acts as a brace against these various faults and makes the whole swinging action easier to perform correctly.

By a tight grip we also mean with practically all the fingers that are on the club. These would be the last three, principally, of the left hand and the first three of the right. Many players have a tendency to place the forefinger of the right hand, the one that hooks around the shaft just below the right thumb, very lightly on the club. Don't do it. Hook this finger around the shaft firmly, so that the tip of it makes a definite contact with the tip of the thumb. If you don't, the club will be liable to drop, at the top of the swing, into the big V between the forefinger and thumb. This means a loss of control at the top, which must be regained as the club comes down.

So much for the grip—a tight two-knuckle overlap, to reduce it to capsule form.

Now, how do we stand up the ball? No great mystery is involved in this either, although certain points must be observed.

In the first place, we should take a position that enables us to swing the club back freely and to bring it down to the ball on an inside-out arc easily. For this the weight should be about equally divided between the feet. The knees must be slightly flexed, better too much than too little. The body should be bent slightly from the waist but the shoulders should be rounded or hunched over. The head should be down, not to an exaggerated extent, but down rather than up. The right shoulder, of course, will be lower than the left, because the right hand is farther down on the shaft than the left hand.

How We Stand

The feet, quite naturally, come in for plenty of attention. How far apart should they be? What is their position in relation to the direction line? Which way should they point? And should the weight be forward, on the balls of the feet, or backward, on the heels?

It is generally agreed now that the feet should be about as far apart as the width of the shoulders—the feet at the instep, that is. This is wide enough for good balance, and balance is important in getting ready to swing the club. Bob Jones used an abnormally narrow stance. He liked it because with it he could get the full hip turn that he wanted on the backswing. Jones had a bigger hip turn than most of the good golfers of his day, or since. There were others in the Jones and pre-Jones eras, though, who took very wide stances, particularly some of the early British stars. In fact, at that time, stances and swings generally varied a great deal more than they do now.

As to the feet in relation to the direction line, use the square stance (Fig. 7A). That is, have the feet an equal distance from the line, especially for any full shot with a No. 5 iron up to a driver. With a square stance the average person will have enough freedom for a backswing which is full, and for a forward swing that is free.

The closed stance, with the right foot withdrawn a couple of inches farther from the direction line than the left, makes it easier to get the full backswing, probably with a flattened plane, but tends to restrict the forward swing. The open stance, with the left foot drawn back farther than the right, has the opposite effect, restricting the backswing and forcing it into a more upright position, but facilitating the forward swing (Fig. 7B).

You will be able to work into the open and closed stances

later, using them for certain shots and to influence a particular swing you want. But while you are learning the method given here, content yourself with the square stance. It presents no problems and requires no adjustments.

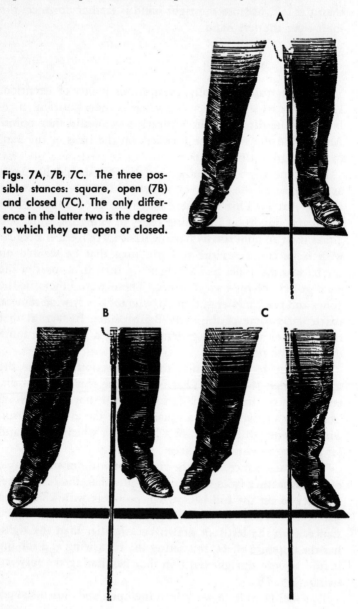

Figs. 7A, 7B, 7C. The three possible stances: square, open (7B) and closed (7C). The only difference in the latter two is the degree to which they are open or closed.

Neither foot, we believe, should be exactly perpendicular to the direction line. Both should be pointed outward somewhat, the left more than the right. Here the rest of the player's body should be considered. Like the open and closed stance, the position of the feet has a tendency to influence the back and forward swings. A right foot that is perpendicular to the line will restrict the backswing. A person with a big trunk and heavy shoulders is liable to have trouble getting the club back far enough. For him, to make things easier, we would definitely point the right foot somewhat to the right.

The pointing of the left foot to the left is a natural action, one of the few in this game. This position makes swinging through the ball easier, and, so long as the swing is in the right direction, we certainly don't want to do anything that impedes it.

There is a strong tendency in almost anybody, in taking his stance, to get his weight forward, on the balls of his feet. This is natural, because the body is bent forward and the shoulders hunched over.

But don't let the weight get forward. Keep it evenly balanced, so far as you can, between the ball and heel of each foot, slightly favoring the heel. This little point, small as it is, has a decided effect on the swing. Since it isn't a natural action, you will have to consciously check it as you take your stance, until it becomes an established habit. Its importance lies in the fact that when the weight is forward we tend to take the club back in a more upright arc, which we don't want. When the weight is more on the heels, the flatter plane that we do want comes easier. With the weight forward there is a tendency, too, to get the swing outside the line on the way down, a disastrous action.

The position of the arms, particularly the elbows, also is is a part of the stance. We do not want loose arms or elbows that crook and point outward, left and right. These lead to a loose and sloppy swing (Fig. 8).

The arms should be very nearly straight, though by no means locked. The elbows, especially, should be pointed down toward the ground, not out to the sides. You will notice, if you put the elbows in this position, that the very act of doing it brings the arms and the elbows closer together. This is where we want them.

Beware the "Open" Body

Now for the "open" body, cited earlier. There is a natural
reason for this. It occurs unconsciously, because our right
hand is lower on the shaft than our left. As we reach slightly
lower with our right hand to grip the club, our right shoulder moves down and forward slightly and our right hip
moves forward just a little bit. Slight as they are, these

Fig. 8. Elbow depressions up. If
we make it a point to keep these
little hollows on the inside of the
elbows pointing up rather than in,
our arms are brought closer together and the swing is likely to
be more compact.

movements "open" our body to the ball. You can see the
effect more easily if you drop your right hand a foot down
the shaft from the left. This, by exaggerating the action,
opens the body much more. It is just another of the natural
actions we make in golf which are wrong.

The effect of this "opening" is threefold. It causes us to
aim to the left, restricts our backswing and shoulder turn,
and puts us in a position to hit from the outside in before
we have even started the club back. Heaven knows it is hard
enough for the average player to swing from the inside
without taking a preparatory position that almost prevents it.

You can have a friend check your position at address by holding a club against the front of your shoulders and see-

Fig. 9A. The "open body" stance, a common fault, with the body slouched and turned a little too easily toward the target. Note that the shaft of the club points to the right of the player's trousers fly.

ing where the club points. It will point to the left of the target an amazing number of times. To bring it around so that it points toward the target or parallel to the direction line requires a conscious effort with the hips and shoulders. But that effort must be made until it becomes a firmly established habit. For one who has been addressing the ball with an "open" body for a long time, the squaring around will seem awkward. For a while he will think he is looking at the target over the point of his left shoulder. This thought, in fact, is a good one to have. It will almost serve as a check point.

For men there is another and surer check point. At address the hips should be so positioned, parallel to the direction line, that as the player looks down, the fly of his trousers is to the right of the club shaft by two inches. If his hips are "open," the fly and the club will be in the same line, or the fly even a little to the left. Women wearing shorts or slacks can make the same check on the center seam. Women in skirts are out of luck on this one unless there is a pleat or some other decorative line directly down the front of the skirt (Fig. 9).

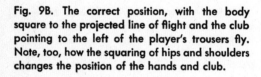

Fig. 9B. The correct position, with the body square to the projected line of flight and the club pointing to the left of the player's trousers fly. Note, too, how the squaring of hips and shoulders changes the position of the hands and club.

One more point about the hips. Don't let them stick out to the rear. You are not a circus clown waiting to be whacked with a board. Tall people with long backs, especially sway-backs, are liable to do this. We want the *derrière* directly under the trunk, pushed forward a little, if anything.

The squaring around of the hips and shoulders is more difficult if the foot stance is open. It is easier when the foot stance is square, easiest of all when the stance is closed. That is why, as a matter of fact, it is easier to hook a ball from a closed stance than from an open one. The club is coming farther from the inside because the body is square to the ball, or facing a shade to the right.

We have had pupils with pretty good swings who found it almost impossible to take a straight divot, for instance. They persisted in swinging from the outside. Once they were shown the little trick of squaring their hips and shoulders, the straight divot, and even the inside-out divot, came easily.

So be certain you are not deliberately handicapping yourself before you start by "opening" your body to the ball. The misalignment is slight but the effect is great.

How Far from the Ball?

Next comes the question of how far to stand from the ball. There is general agreement we should not reach for it. Byron Nelson has said that it is easy to stand too far away but impossible to stand too close. This is an exaggeration. If we stand very close to the ball the proximity cramps our swing and forces it to too upright a plane. A flatter plane is more desirable, and we will not get it if we crowd the ball. If we stand very close we get the feeling that there is not room for our hands to go through. This tends to throw us outside, where there is plenty of room but also ruination.

It is very easy, though, to stand too far away. In fact the tendency is to do exactly this. The average player, once he gets the idea that he must hit the ball from the inside out, promptly moves farther from the ball so he'll make it easier to come from the inside. This is a fallacy, of course, but that's what he does. If you speak to him about it, he may even throw Jim Turnesa at you. Turnesa stands farther from the ball than any other top-rank professional, and Jim won the PGA championship in 1952.

We have no quarrel with Turnesa; let him stand where he will. But for the average player it is a fact that standing an abnormal distance from the ball makes him bend and reach to hit it. He bends at the waist and he gets his hands too far from his body. He will also invariably move his weight forward onto the balls of his feet.

All this is wrong. He thinks he is giving himself plenty of room to bring the club head to the ball from the inside. Actually, every move he has made is one that tends to make him throw the club from the top and hit the ball from the outside. The pronounced bend at the waist, the distance of the hands from the body, and the weight pitched forward —each alone is an invitation to throw from the top. All three put together make such a disastrous move almost a certainty.

How, then, do we know what is the right distance? Well,

strange to say, your club, if it is the standard 43-inch driver, will tell you. Measure the length of the grip. It will be about 11 inches. Next measure from the lower end of the grip to the little colored plastic band or collar which the manufacturer has put at the top of the hosel. You will find that the distance is 28 inches. This is the length of the bare or naked part of the shaft.

If you are from 5 feet 10 inches to 6 feet 4 inches tall, the length of this naked shaft is the distance you should stand from the ball for a drive. And by *distance* we mean the distance from the tee to a line drawn from the tip of one toe to the tip of the other.

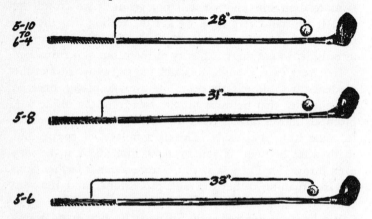

Fig. 10. Checking your distance from the ball. Shows how easy it is to measure the distance you should stand from the ball, depending on your height.

Simple, isn't it? Almost too simple to be true, but that's the way it works out for the vast majority of players of average build using the normal driver. Adjustments have to be made, of course, for persons with abnormally long or short arms and those with big waistlines. But the basic formula is sound. Lower your driver to the ground with the hosel collar at the tee and place your feet so that the line from toe to toe is where the grip begins. You should now be about 28 inches from the ball (Fig. 10).

Players shorter than 5 feet 10 will stand farther away, persons taller than 6 feet 4 will stand closer, with the same standard-length driver. A person 5 feet 8, for example, will stand about 31 inches from the ball; one 5 feet 6 will stand about 33 inches from it.

The formula holds for the other wooden clubs too, the Nos. 2, 3, and 4, in which the length of the naked shaft shortens slightly with each, and with each of which we stand a little closer to the ball.

Unfortunately, no such measuring rod can be used for the irons. The shorter the iron, the closer we stand to the ball, but in varying degrees. For instance, a person 6 feet 2 will stand a distance from the ball which is about $1\frac{1}{2}$ inches less than the length of the naked shaft with a 2 iron. But for a 9 iron he will stand a distance of more than 5 inches less than the shaft length.

For the 7 iron, a favorite for practice, for loosening up, and for instruction, we have given the approximate distances for persons of different heights in the following table.

Fortunately for the convenience of the formula, all the leading club manufacturers have used the same length for their driver grips—11 inches—for several years. If at some time in the future they change, the convenience would be affected but the distance we stand from the ball would not change. Knowing what the distance should be, it would be simple enough to measure it on our club and put a mark of some kind on the grip or the shaft, depending on which was affected.

DISTANCES FROM BALL

Driver		No. 7 Iron	
Height	*Distance*	*Height*	*Distance*
5 feet 6	33 inches	5 feet 6	20 inches
5 feet 8	31 inches	5 feet 8	19 inches
5 feet 10	28 inches	5 feet 10	18 inches
6 feet	28 inches	6 feet	18 inches
6 feet 2	28 inches	6 feet 2	18 inches
6 feet 4	28 inches	6 feet 4	18 inches

These distances, we repeat, will be altered by arm length and girth. Otherwise, they are a reliable guide for persons of normal build.

Where We Put the Ball

Now that we have determined how we should grip the club

and how we should stand to swing it, only one question remains in these preparatory maneuvers: Where shall we place the ball?

For the normal drive the ball is teed opposite the instep of the left foot. The position is this far to the left because the ball must be struck at the bottom of the arc of the swing. The bottom of this arc occurs not at a point midway between the feet, but about opposite the left instep or left heel. It is here because the body's center of gravity is moved to the left at the beginning of the downswing by a pronounced shift of weight from the right leg to the left. The left leg is the chief supporter of weight when the club hits the ball. Therefore the bottom of the arc is opposite the left foot. It's no more complicated than that.

We do not intend to make a big deal of ball placement for the other clubs. This has been done in some systems of instruction, with a definite and different spot prescribed for each club in the bag. This is ridiculous. Such hairsplitting gives the pupil the uneasy feeling that if he doesn't have the ball in exactly the right spot he cannot make the shot. Nonsense.

For the other clubs below the driver, the ball is brought back to the right, slightly. But never farther, for a normal shot, than the center point between the feet. As we use the more lofted clubs they get shorter and our feet are placed closer together. But right down to the most lofted club we do not play the ball back farther than the midpoint for a normal shot.

We would, therefore, advise playing all irons from the 9 to the 5, exactly midway between the heels. For the 2, 3, and 4 irons, play the ball about halfway between this midpoint and the left heel. We would play the fairway woods about opposite the left heel and the driver opposite the left instep (Fig. 11).

We realize that some of the touring pros have advised playing the ball about opposite the left heel for all shots and merely moving the right foot closer to the left as the clubs rise in number. This is fine for the pros, who move into the ball so well on all shots. But the average player doesn't move nearly that well. It is much easier for him to get the more lofted irons through the ball with a descending club-head arc if the ball is at the midpoint position.

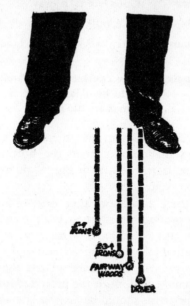

Fig. 11. Where to place the ball. The four basic positions: for the driver, for the fairway woods, for the long irons, for the medium and short irons.

With this we complete the preparatory moves, the actions and positions you take—and avoid taking—as you get ready to swing the club.

You have found, to sum up briefly, that you take a tight, two-knuckle, overlapping grip and that this grip, so far as contact with the club is concerned, is a combination palm-and-finger grip with the left hand and an all-finger grip with the right. We have also made it clear that once this grip is welded to the shaft of the club at the address, it does not change or loosen from the time the club leaves the ball on the backswing until the finish of the follow-through.

A second point you have learned is how to stand to the ball—how far apart your feet should be, how your weight should be distributed, that you bend only slightly from the waist but that you hunch your shoulders, and, finally, how far you should stand from the ball and where the ball itself should be.

4 The Backswing

Fatal flaw	Open-face take-away.
Awful results	Slice, pull, smother, hook, scuff, or shank.
Magic move	Early backward wrist break, with thumb press.
Check points	One knuckle of left hand visible, two of right hand, and none of club face when hands are hip high.

Now you are ready to start the swing, to uncover the first fatal flaws that appear, with the horrible shots they produce, and to learn the first of the magic moves that will cut strokes from your score.

Ironically, these first flaws that creep into the average player's swing produce an effect that is the exact opposite of what he wants. Just as you have, he has read and heard all his golfing life that certain things are essential. The first of these is that you must pivot, the second is that the club must be taken away from the ball inside the projected line of flight, the third is that the wrists should be broken late and upward.

We dealt with these three points individually in Chapter 2. Now let's see what happens when you put them into practice. You twist your body as you start the take-away. This brings the club back on an inside line. Fine. It opens the face of the club too. Excellent, you say, for you know it should be open at the top of the swing. You delay the wrist break as long as possible and then let the wrists break upward.

Then what happens? The very thing you wanted most to avoid. You hit the ball from the outside in, with an open face (usually), and you get an outlandish slice If you close the face on the downswing you probably will get a pull, or a smother (if it's closed too much), or a hook. If the club is outside the line far enough, you will even get that most horrible of all shots, a shank.

You are then thoroughly crestfallen. You have done everything you'd been told to do and you still hit those awful shots. Why?

You hit them because your early movement got you into such a position at the top that you could hardly hit anything else.

Your early pivot, your attempt to "turn in a barrel," didn't permit you to transfer your weight to your right leg. You kept too much of it on your left leg.

Taking the club away inside (it was probably quite sharply inside) got it moving too flat, as well as opening the face.

Then, to get the swing farther along, you had to bring the club up. At that point things began to get tight and uncomfortable. To ease them you stopped the turn that your shoulders were making and let your left wrist collapse, or bend back and go under the club. This let you raise the club and get what you felt was a full swing, without being uncomfortable. The face of the club, of course, was wide open at the top. (See Fig. 20.)

What happened next was inevitable. You started the downswing by regripping with your left hand, which had loosened, which made you get the club head started moving too soon. Your weight, being mostly on your left leg, moved back to the right leg. You turned your hips and shoulders sharply, which threw the club onto the outside-in line you were trying to avoid. And you came down across the ball. Chances are that as you did, your left knee snapped back and locked and your right knee bent straight out in front of you. And your follow-through, what there was of it, carried the club around you instead of up and out after the ball.

You, however, see none of these things as the cause of your bad shots. You feel only that you haven't done well enough what you are trying to do, and in your efforts to meet the standards, you exaggerate the actions. You don't improve. You may easily get worse. And you finally end your practice session frustrated and dejected, or your round, if you are playing, with a shameful score.

The Magic Move *

Fortunately, there is a cure for all this, a cure that is almost miraculous. The magic move that puts you on the right track immediately is simply this:

*Start the backswing with an early backward wrist break.

* The early wrist-break, or pre-set position, was described as "the swing of the future" by Gary Wiren, director of education of the national PGA, in an article in Golf Shop Operations, March 1976.

Of course this sounds too simple to be true. It violates every rule you ever heard about starting the swing. Your first reaction is that Messers. Dante and Elliott have gone completely off their rockers. But it is true—and unless your swing is now everything that you want it to be, you will find out how and why this magic move is made.

The wrist break itself is simple enough, actually, though if you have been breaking in the conventional way you may need a little time to convince yourself of what is to be done and to make yourself do it.

Since the backward break is one of the key points in our system, let's be absolutely certain you understand what it is.

First, hold your right hand in front of you, fingers together and extended, thumb up and the palm squarely facing the left. From that position bend the hand to the right, trying to make the fingers come back toward the outside of the wrist. You can't get them anywhere near the wrist, of course, but a person with supple wrists can bend the hand back until hand and wrist form a right angle (Fig. 12).

This motion of the hand, straight back, is the backward wrist break.

Fig. 12. The way the right hand should move from the wrist in the early backward break—straight back toward the outside of the forearm, with no turning or rolling.

The standard wrist break is quite different. Hold your hand again as you held it before. Now, instead of bending it backward, bend it up, so that the thumb comes toward you. That is the orthodox, accepted wrist break. Forget it. You will get it eventually, but you don't want it now.

You will remember that the grip we stipulated was one which, at address, showed only two knuckles of the left hand

and one of the right hand. You will also recall that the right hand was put on the club so that the left thumb lay right down the middle of the right palm. This brought the heel of the right hand against the big knuckle at the base of the left thumb.

The Thumb Press

To make the backward wrist break we merely push the heel of the right hand down against the big knuckle of the left thumb. This is a downward pressure of the heel on the thumb. When it is done, without moving the hands other-

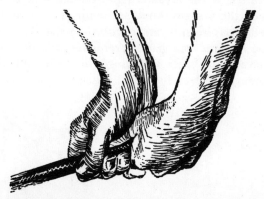

Fig. 13A. How the backward break is made, with the heel of the right hand pressing down on the knuckle of the left thumb. The back of the left hand begins to turn down and under.

Fig. 13B. How *not* to make the break. Wrists and hands have rolled, the back of the left hand has turned upward. The right hand is rolling too, instead of bending straight back.

wise, the right hand breaks backward at the wrist and the left hand breaks forward or inward, the back of the left hand going under and facing, in a general way, toward the ground (Fig. 13).

At this point the club will have come back slightly inside the projected line of flight but the club face will not have opened. The face will be at about a 45-degree angle with the ground and, as you stand there, you will not be able to see any of it (Fig. 14A).

To be certain you are making the break correctly there is a perfect check point at this stage. If you look at your hands you will see, if the break is right, one knuckle of your left hand and the first two knuckles of the right. The left hand will be broken in, at an angle with the wrist (Fig. 15).

If the break is completed here, *without letting the hands move away from their address position,* the club will have been brought back and up until it is almost parallel with the

Fig. 14A. How the backward break looks from the side. Note the bend in the left wrist as the back of the hand turns down, and the position of the right wrist. Notice also that the face of the club has not opened.

ground. How near it approaches the parallel depends on how supple your wrists happen to be.

Following our description of how the break is made, try it ten times. If you don't soon get the feel of it, try it twenty or fifty times. But do it until you get the feel, checking yourself each time with the left-hand and right-hand knuckles and the angle of the face of the club.

This is a key move—the foundation of the swing—and you must do it right, get the feel of doing it right, and do it so much that it becomes automatic. It is easy to practice, requiring very little room, and can be worked on indoors or out, winter as well as summer. Get it, and get it right.

We have not put this into the actual swing yet, remember. We are still working on the mechanics of the wrist break. It is just possible that at this fundamental stage you will refuse to believe that you can hit the ball with such a break. So make this test:

Fig. 14B. The wrong break, with wrists rolled. Note the difference in the left-hand position here and in Fig. 14A, and observe also the differences in the club-face positions. Never do it like this.

Go to the practice tee, or to a range or an indoor net. Address the ball. Make the backward break and do nothing else Don't shift your weight, move your hips, or turn your shoulders. Just make the backward break. Hold it a couple of seconds. Now simply turn your shoulders, letting the shoulders swing your arms and the club up to the top, and then go right on through with the swing and hit the ball.

You will be amazed at what happens after you try this a few times. You will find, if you keep the wrist position, that you not only hit the ball, but that you hit it solidly, hit it straight, and hit it a surprising distance.

You will also discover that the more you permit the *turning shoulders* to swing the club up, the better you will hit the ball and the farther you will hit it. Make no effort to swing the arms; just let the shoulders move them and the club. The more the arms are swung independently of the shoulders, the less likely you are to reach a good position

Fig. 15. Here is what you should see when you make the backward break perfectly—only one knuckle of the left hand but two knuckles of the right.

at the top. So picture the shoulders as the motivating force, the "motor."

The closer you bring this motivating force to the axis of the swing (the spinal column) the better the swing will be.

This two-piece action is invaluable for practicing the immediate break, for getting the feel of the break, for checking whether you have done it correctly or not, and for proving to yourself its value and the value of the hand-and-wrist position. In fact, you can use it in actual play. We have pupils who do.

Into the Swing

The next step is to incorporate the early wrist break into the swing itself, making it a single uninterrupted motion. For this we must start with what has come to be known as the forward press, for it is with this that the backswing begins.

The forward press is simply a device that gets us from the passive into the active stage smoothly, without a jerk. Standing in a stationary position, even for a few seconds, is tiring. Ask any service man who has stood at attention for any extended period. We don't pass easily from a stationary position into a big move. The trick in golf is to go from the stationary position of address to the big movement of the backswing without a jerky effort. The forward press provides this transition. It is the little move that leads into the big one.

It can be done in several ways, with the right knee, with the hips, with the hands, with a turn of the hips. We want a lateral movement of the hips, no turn. It is a slight pushing of the hips to the left, laterally, about an inch or two. This press is in the opposite direction from the big move. But as the hips come back from their little pushing motion, they

Fig. 16. The backward break off the forward press. The "ghost" hands show position as the press is completed. The backward break begins as the hands move past the player's right leg.

keep right on sliding and go into a lateral turning motion to the right—the beginning of the backswing—and we are off. This makes for the smoothest transition of all.

As the hips move to the left in the press, they pull the hands with them, just slightly, only a fraction of an inch. When the hips come back, the hands come back.

Now, as the hips and hands come back from the press, *push the heel of the right hand down firmly but not sharply, on the left thumb.* The back of the left hand starts to turn under—and the all-important backward wrist break has begun (Fig. 16).

This move should not be a sharp or violent action. It is not an instant break. It is an early, swinging break. It feels quicker than it actually is.

Fig. 17A. The completed break, with left arm parallel with ground. Big shoulder turn. Club face is square.

Fig. 17B. A common fault in executing the break. The left shoulder has ducked, the player substituting the duck for the correct turning action.

The hands and arms, meanwhile, have moved to the right as the wrists were cocking, and the hips were sliding into a lateral turn. Before you realize it your left arm will be parallel with the ground. *And at that point the wrist-break should be complete!*

Fig. 17C. The wrong break altogether. Player has not broken backward, but has rolled his wrists and opened the club face wide.

Right here is the first check point. Stop the swing and look at your hands. If the wrist break has been performed correctly you will see at this point just the reverse of what you saw at the address:

You should see only one knuckle of the left hand, but two knuckles of the right hand, those at the bases of the index and middle fingers (Figs. 18 and 19).

You should not be able to see any of the face of the club, either. The face should be turned away from you, not at the 45-degree angle it was in the stationary test, but still turned away.

You should set a definite inward bend of the left hand, a reflex angle formed by the forearm and the back of the hand. The shaft should be at about a 90-degree angle to the ground and the angle formed by the left arm and the shaft of the club should be about a right angle, or less.

You should feel that the wrists cannot be broken any more. They will be, a little, at the top by the weight of the club head, but they should feel now as though the break were absolutely complete.

Fig. 18. What you must see when you turn and look at your hands after the backward break is completed—one knuckle of the left hand, two knuckles of the right, and none of the club face.

If these check points are not all clearly visible (except the club-shaft position) exactly as we have given them, your break has been wrong. The chances are that you have pushed the heel of the right hand *sideways* against the left thumb, instead of *down*. This brings the club too sharply on an inside line, tends to open the face somewhat, and doesn't get the back of the left hand started going down under as it must.

With such a break, when it is completed, you will see two knuckles of the left hand and only one of the right, just as you did at address.

So correct it by starting over again and pushing *down* on the left thumb. That brings the back of the left hand down and under and gives you the position you must have.

What It Does

Heretical, you say? Of course it is. Awkward and uncomfortable? Oh, yes, indeed. But you want to break 80, don't you, or 90, or whatever goal you have set for yourself? Then stick with it. Hit some balls with it, being sure your execution is right, before you condemn it.

Meanwhile, look what it has done for your swing already. The club head has been started almost straight back from the ball, as it should be. The club face has been kept square, as it must be if you are going to play better golf. The hip

Fig. 19. What you will see if you have made the wrong break—two or three knuckles of the left hand, only one of the right, and plenty of the club face.

slide has moved much of your weight over to the right leg, where it must go, and your hips are now turning somewhat. Your right elbow has been automatically brought in against your side, starting you on a tight, controlled arc. The wrist break at the same time has started the swing in a plane that will prove to be ideal, neither too upright nor too flat. The shoulders have begun to turn and to tilt just a little, with the left going down slightly, and the right coming up. And, perhaps most important of all, your hands and wrists are set early in exactly the position they must be in.

All this adds up to the fact that although the backswing has progressed only about two-thirds of its distance, you already are locked into actions which will bring you to the top in perfect position.

Your next questions, without a doubt, are going to be: Why is this first move so important, and why does it do what it does?

To answer these we will have to go back quite a few years in the theories of golf technique. Thirty years ago there was one accepted method of hitting a golf ball. That was with an open face and with a late wrist break. Those were the points the teaching pros taught then—the face should be opened on the backswing, should be open at the top, and should be closed to a square position on the downswing as the ball was hit. The natural way to get the open face at the top was with a late wrist break. The break never should be started before the hands were waist high. In fact, many taught that you should pay no attention whatever to breaking the wrists; they would break by themselves. This is the way Vardon, Jones, Walter Hagen, Gene Sarazen, and most of the others hit the ball. There were exceptions, such as Craig Wood, who won the National Open in 1941, and Lawson Little, who won the Open in 1940 and the American and British Amateur championships twice each, in successive years. Shut-face hitters, both were looked upon as heretics.

After World War II, with competition on the American professional circuit getting ever keener, with ever more money at stake, the pros began to make changes here and there, tinkering with the swing, both for accuracy and for distance. Sam Snead, Byron Nelson, and Ben Hogan made alterations. Then the younger group came along, Arnold Palmer, Bill Casper, and others. They made more.

In 1958 one of the girl pros, Betty Hicks, quoted another pro, Helen Dettweiler, as saying that the men were not practicing what they preached. The men urged their pupils, she said, to sweep the club head low away from the ball and delay the wrist cock until the hands were hip high. But the men themselves, she observed, were with few exceptions starting their wrist cock at the beginning of the backswing, and she offered to produce movies to prove it.

In 1961 the great little West Coast phenomenon and 1961 PGA champion, Jerry Barber, described how he starts his wrist break even earlier—right off the forward press. Sequence pictures showed him doing exactly that. He has the break completed, he said (and again the pictures prove it), by the time his hands are hip high.

It is also noticeable in their pictures that both Palmer and Casper have the club face in a relatively closed position at the top of the swing, not completely shut but closed at least 45 degrees. So do several others, including Wes Ellis, former Canadian, Metropolitan, and Texas Open champion. All are striving for what they consider a square face at the top. With it they know they will bring it square to the line at impact without any manipulation on the downswing. This is something the old-timers had trouble with. Being open at the top, they had to manipulate the club on the way down. Usually they succeeded; quite often they didn't. But that is one reason, we believe, why the modern pros are much more consistent, as well as longer, than their predecessors of thirty years ago.

All of which is background for the action taught in this book. The backward wrist break gives you the square position so necessary for accuracy. The early, swinging wrist break locks you in the square position early.

So the first flaws that spoil a golf swing have been uncovered. You know what they are and the horrible shots they cause. More to the point, you have been given the first of the magic moves that will eliminate those bad shots and put you on the road to better golf and lower scores.

5 *At the Top*

Fatal flaw	Easy-chair slouch.
Awful results	Slice, scuff, smother, shank, pull, hook, top, or sky.
Magic move	Steel-spring tension with straight left wrist.
Check points	Two knuckles of left hand visible, one knuckle of right; 45-degree angle for club face; shoulder tap for plane.

At the end of the last chapter we had taken you through the first movement of the backswing, the early, swinging backward wrist break. That set the hands and wrists and the face of the club in the proper positions, locked them in, as it were. It also brought the left arm parallel with the ground.

The next movement is the one that takes us to the top of the swing. This is a vital position, and when it is reached the next fatal flaw makes its appearance.

It might be well to first take a general look at the top of the backswing. Actually there is no absolute top, in the sense that everything which has been moving in one upward and backward direction reaches its limit at the same time and starts forward and down together. All the parts of the swinging system—the club, hands, arms, body, and legs— do not reach their backward limits at the same time. They reach them in a steady progression, from the ground up. The knees get there first, followed by the hips, then the shoulders, the arms, the hands, and finally the club head.

There is quite a time gap, too, between the extension limits of the first three parts and the last three. There is a similar lag in the time they start down, too. Swings of the top professionals vary somewhat, of course, but sequence pictures never fail to show that the knees, hips, and shoulders reach the end of their backward movements well before the arms, hands, and club head. The same pictures invariably show the knees and hips moving into the downswing before the upper part of the body. In fact, the knees and hips are actually moving into the downswing before the club head has gone all the way back.

This, however, is something you do not have to worry about or even think of. Since it is a reflex action, it will take place without your knowledge.

When we speak of the top of the backswing here, we mean the top of the swing for the hands.

The Fatal Flaw

You have just seen, in the previous chapter, how the swing can be thrown off and a bad position reached at the top by an early body-twist with a late upward wrist break. A swing that starts out pretty well can also be ruined as it nears the top. It happens repeatedly in the common, orthodox swing and it can happen with the swing we are giving you. Nobody is immune to it. It is a position we call the easy-chair slouch.

It happens this way. As the swing goes up toward the top, the whole swinging system gets tighter and a definite tension develops. This is felt mostly in the upper part of the body, the shoulders, the left arm, and the left hand. It is not a comfortable feeling. To ease it the player subconsciously checks the shoulder turn, lets the left hand bend backward as the wrist collapses, and loosens the left-hand grip. He's heard a thousand times that he should be loose and relaxed and comfortable, so he's going to be. Often, he even bends his left arm (Fig. 21) .

Instantly every good, sound element of the swing disappears. The restriction of the shoulder turn and the collapse of the left wrist permit the player to bring the club up instead of back and around. The bending back of the left hand puts the left wrist under the shaft at the top and opens the face of the club. The relaxed left-hand grip lets the club drop down into an overswing. The arc of the swing is narrowed and the plane is elevated. The right elbow comes up, and generally more weight settles on the left leg, as the player pivots instead of moving his weight, and settles himself into a more comfortable position—the easy-chair slouch (Fig. 21).

Just about every available handicap has now been pro-

68

Figs. 20A, 20B. The open-face take-away (described in Chapter 4) that leads to so much trouble. In A the player has taken the club away from the ball with very little break, has rolled the face open, and is taking the club around his body. In B it is going around and low, and the player is getting a tight, uncomfortable feeling.

duced to prevent a good downswing. The awful result is a succession of horrible shots which almost defy description. The ball can fly anywhere. Most often it will slice. But it can also be pulled, smothered, hooked, scuffed, topped, skied, or shanked.

The slice will come from two actions: the open face and the outside-in swing that this fellow cannot help but deliver. If he manages to get the face square to the path the club is following, the shot will be a pull. If he gets the face a little closed, he will hook. If he gets it hooded, he will smother the ball. Some players will even turn the face completely over so that they make contact with the ball partly on the top of the club head, where white ball marks will show. They will pop the ball up, or sky it. Since their weight transference is almost sure to be bad, with most of it behind the ball at impact, they can either hit behind the ball or, just missing the ground at the bottom of the swing arc, top the ball as the swing begins to rise. And if their outside-in swing gets far enough outside, they will shank.

Fig. 21. What the bad backswing leads to—the "easy-chair slouch." The player eased the tight, uncomfortable feeling he was getting in Fig. 20B by relaxing his shoulders, bringing the club up, bending his left arm, and letting his left hand fall back, opening the club face wide. He'll never hit a good one from here.

A   B

Figs. 22A, 22B. The correct backswing. In A the backward wrist break is well under way and the club face is square. In B the position is getting tighter as the club is brought around and up, the wrist position has been retained, and the club face kept square.

The only bad shot this fellow will not make, is a push—a straight ball to the right of the target. That shot can only come with an inside-out swing, and our horrible example will never have that, with the position he was in at the top.

With bad shots coming almost inevitably and a good shot a complete accident, our player here is going to pile up strokes at a rapid rate. He will not only get fives and sixes on many holes, he will get a few eights and nines. Yet, when he finally comes in with his 102, he will blame everything but the fatal flaw which was responsible. He will never realize (unless his pro tells him) what he was doing.

The Magic Move

The move that avoids the easy-chair slouch and gets you to the top correctly is simply a purposeful shoulder turn with a firm retention of the wrist position gained by the backward break.

When the backward break was completed the left arm was parallel with the ground. It could well be completed earlier. But at whatever point, the arms, club and shoulders have worked up good momentum. So just let the shoulders continue to turn and move the swing to the top. Remember, the shoulders are the motivating force (Fig. 22).

The top of the swing, for the hands, is at a level just about even with the top of the head. If you make sure the shoulders turn a full 90 degrees, the hands will reach that level.

A point which must be stressed here is that the shoulders must *turn* on the backswing, not rock. As the hands are brought up and around, the shoulders will tilt somewhat, with the right eventually becoming higher than the left. But one of the worst things that can happen is for the left shoulder to duck. When this occurs the club goes off the plane it should follow. It comes up. And when it comes up the hand position gained by the wrist break is lost. The left wrist goes under the shaft and the face of the club opens.

Many players, we find in teaching, will duck the left shoulder and think they are turning it. They substitute the duck for the turn. When they do, they get themselves in a perfect position at the top to come down across the ball from the outside—even to shank it.

The magic move here is not an action. It is a position—the right position at the top. That position is measured in several ways: by the weight on the right leg, by the shoulder turn, by the unmoved head, but most of all by the tightness of the coil, the hand-and-wrist position, the face of the club, and the plane of the swing.

Most important is the firm retention of the hand-and-wrist position gained by the backward wrist break. If it is held, it almost forces you into the right position at the top. This is one of its greatest values (Fig. 23) .

Holding that wrist position requires effort, though, because as the windup proceeds, the tension and the stretching increase and your strong instinct is to relieve it. *You must not relieve it.*

A good backward wrist break feels stiff and awkward. That

Fig. 23. Keeping everything tight, player has reached the top in perfect position. Note the full shoulder turn, the straight left arm, the unbroken left wrist, the right hand under the shaft, the club face still square. He's ready to make the right move down to the ball.

is the feeling you must continue to have as the swing goes to the top. If you don't do anything to ease it, to fall into the easy-chair slouch, such as collapsing the left wrist, ducking the left shoulder, or opening the left hand, the swing will continue in the plane we want it, which is a little on the flat side. In this plane, if the club is to get back to a position horizontal with the ground, the shoulders must turn fully. There is no other way to get it there.

If this is done properly—just a stubborn retention of the wrist break and a full turn of the shoulders—you will reach the top in a stretched, spring-steel tight position, poised and ready to deliver a powerful swing at the ball. The left heel will be off the ground slightly, at least 60 per cent of the weight will be on the right leg, the hips will be turned about 45 degrees, the shoulders at least 90 degrees, the left arm will be straight, the grip tight, the right wrist will be under the shaft, and the clubface will be at about a 45-degree angle with the ground, maybe a little more.

With the right wrist under the shaft the right hand will be weakened by being bent back, but the left hand will be strengthened because hand, wrist, and forearm will be in a straight line. This so-called straight-left-wrist position is important because it gives strength where strength is needed.

A Straight Left Wrist

One of our women pupils, and she was typical of many, used to insist when she was learning to swing, that she could not hold the club tight at the top with the straight-left-wrist position. She wanted her left wrist under the shaft and claimed that was the only way she could hold the club tight.

She was wrong, of course, but she had to be convinced. So we had her hold the club in her left hand alone, in front of her, as tightly as she could. Then we bent her left hand backward and took the club away. It was easy, because with her hand bent backward, the fingers automatically opened and her grip weakened. The same thing happens when the hand is bent forward; the fist cannot be clenched tight.

But when the back of that woman's hand and her wrist were in a straight line, you could not take the club away from her without the use of a considerable amount of force.

Fig. 24. If you stop the swing here and look at your hands, you should see only two knuckles of the left hand, one of the right, and either a straight line along the back of the left hand and wrist or even a slight inward bend of the left hand, with the right hand firmly under the shaft.

Actually, one reason she wanted the left wrist under the shaft was so the club could rest in her left hand. Men have the same idea. They can open the fingers a little and the club will still be supported by the palm of the left hand and the thumb.

The strongest possible position is when the wrist and the back of the left hand are in a straight line.

How, you may wonder, can you yourself tell whether you are in the right position at the top? Without a friend to help you, you cannot tell about such things as the amount of hip and shoulder turn. But there are ways to inform yourself of others.

For instance, you can turn your head and look at your hands. If the left wrist has not collapsed you will see two knuckles of that hand, no more than two. If you see three it will mean the left wrist has collapsed. You should also see only one knuckle of the right hand (Fig. 24).

You can check the tightness of your grip by the feel of it.

You can check how close your right arm is to your side by the old test of the balled handkerchief stuck into your right armpit. Only use a small handkerchief; anyone can hold a big one. *If you can hold the small handkerchief, your arm is close enough.* If it drops out, something is wrong.

The Shoulder Tap

One of the hardest things to determine, you might think, is the proper plane of the swing. Is it too flat, or is it too upright? There is an easy way to tell. Take your swing but as you near the top, loosen the grip enough to let the club keep moving back until it hits you. *If it strikes you on the point of your right shoulder, the plane is correct.* If it hits you on the upper arm, the plane is too flat, and if it strikes you on the neck or anywhere between the point of the shoulder and the neck, it is too upright. We call this the shoulder-tap test (Fig. 25).

The position at the top of the backswing is important. If it is reached correctly it means you are halfway through the swing correctly. It means that now, at least, you are in a position to make a good downswing and hit a good shot. With most of our pupils we can tell pretty well, as can any pro, whether a shot will be good or bad just from their position at the top. The position is not an infallible guarantee that the shot will be either good or bad. But a good shot very often follows a good position and a bad shot a bad position. At least with a good position you are ready to hit a good shot. With a bad position you are not.

The flaws we have turned up so far, and the moves and positions we have taught you in getting to the top of the swing, have dealt mostly with the position of the club face. The grip and the stance did. So did the first move away from the ball, with the early backward wrist break and the retention of the wrist position to the top of the swing.

The magic moves so far have been mostly concerned, in a word, with direction. And direction is not only half of the long game but perhaps the "bigger" half; there's not much trouble, as a rule, straight out in front of the tee. The swing taught here, which might be called the Square Face System, produces direction. We have a pupil, an elderly but vigorous owner of a sports establishment, who played good golf for years using the old orthodox methods. He now swears by the magic moves, because, as he says, "I always hit the ball straight. Even when I miss a shot I miss it straight."

But golf is decidedly a coin with two sides. If the position of the club face at impact is one side, the speed of the club

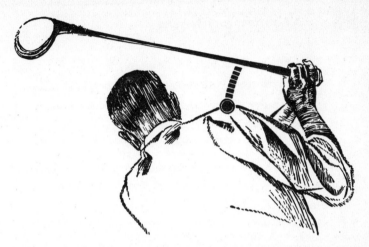

Fig. 25. If we loosen our grip at the top of the swing and let the club drop until it touches us, we feel it tap us on the point of the right shoulder. The shoulder tap establishes the correct plane of the swing. If the club taps us nearer our neck, the swing is too upright. If it touches us on the arm below the shoulder point, the plane is too flat.

head at impact is the other. As we have moved toward the position at the top of the swing we have also gradually become concerned with the speed of the club head.

At the top you have been brought into a position from which you can easily bring the face of the club square to the line at impact and bring it with great speed and from the right direction. The tightness of the grip and of the whole swinging system, the plane of the swing, and the position of the weight—considerably on the right leg—have prepared you to deliver a hard, authoritative swing at the ball.

This is the value of the top-of-the-swing position. Having reached this position, you are well on your way to reducing drastically the number of bad shots you will hit. The next move, the downswing, is the payoff.

6   *Starting Down*

Fatal flaw	Sunday duffer spin.
Awful results	Pull, slice, hook, smother, or shank.
Magic move	Lateral hip slide, with head back.
Check points	One knuckle of left hand visible, two of right hand; right arm touching side.

We have now reached the most important and critical area of golf—the first movement of the downswing. With it

A   B

we uncover the most common and at the same time most devastating flaws.

The golf swing itself is probably the most difficult and certainly the most elusive action in all athletics. Beyond question it is the most frustrating, and nowhere more so than at this very point, where the club and the body make their first moves down toward the ball.

The peak of frustration is reached here because, no matter what has gone before it, this one move can make a greater difference in the result of the swing and the shot than any other.

We can have a perfect grip, start back from the ball properly, reach the top in faultless position—and then ruin it all by the next move we make. Not only *can* the swing be ruined by this move, it *is* ruined about 95 per cent of the time.

The Fatal Flaws

The deadly moves, the most fatal flaws, are these:

(1) Spinning the hips without moving the weight laterally, (2) with this spinning motion turning the right shoulder

Figs. 26A, 26B, 26C. The fatal flaws of the downswing—the spinning of the hips without moving the weight, the turning of the right shoulder out high toward the ball, the lagging of the hands, and the early expenditure of the wrist cock. Result: a weak slap at the ball.

C

high toward the ball, and (3) trying to move the club head or slowing down the hands.

These moves bring quick disaster by causing two things. They make us hit too soon and they make us hit from the outside in. The first robs us of distance, the second of direction—and what else do we want from a full shot?

Because we hit too soon, the drive that might have gone 220 yards goes only 190, and into that trap that juts out into the fairway.

Because we hit from the outside instead of from the inside, the ball is pulled, and, if the face of the club is not square, it will be hooked or sliced, or perhaps smothered or even shanked. The best we can hope for is that we will slice it

78

only a little and that, after starting to the left, it will curve back into the fairway. Even if we are that lucky, we will know we have hit a weak and sloppy shot.

These are the actions and these are the shots that we see on every private course in the country, every public course,

Figs. 27A, 27B, 27C. The magic moves. In A, notice how weight is moving to left as hips move laterally and don't spin. In B, observe how quickly right elbow returns to side, compared with the elbow in 26B. See how the right shoulder comes down; it is farther down in C than it is in 26C even though the hands have not moved as far. And notice how the wrist cock is retained. This player is coming down behind the ball; the player in Fig. 26 is coming out and over it. There is a world of difference.

A

and in stall after stall of every driving range. It can truthfully be said that this is the natural way to hit a golf ball—with the Sunday duffer spin. It is also the principal reason that the scores of our millions of players remain so high. These actions in this one area of the swing produce bad shots in such astronomical volume that the short game, no matter how good it is, can't take up more than a little of the slack. We will say without fear of contradiction that a player who makes these moves and still gets around in 86 on a good day would cut ten strokes from his score if he made the right moves.

The Magic Moves

So what are the right moves, the magic moves? They are, simply: (1) Move the hips *laterally* to the left while (2) keeping the head back and (3) making no effort whatever to move the club.

B   C

We cannot emphasize too strongly that the movement of the hips must be *lateral* and not a turning motion. When the hips are moved laterally to the left from the top of the swing, they carry the weight (which has been mostly on the right leg) along. They get it on the left leg where it must be if we are to hit the ball with anything but a weak slap.

That is the first reason we must move the hips laterally. The second reason is that, since we are twisted and wound up tightly at the top, any turning movement of our hips turns our shoulders too. It turns our right shoulder around high and toward the ball. Hence, when we bring the club down, we have to bring it from the outside in.

The hips will turn if they are moved laterally, but they are very liable not to move laterally if they are merely turned. You can prove this to yourself by standing up and moving your hips to the left as far as they will go. As they near the limit of extension, they will turn and you cannot stop them. At the top of the swing, of course, the hips are turned somewhat to the right, maybe 45 degrees, and as you move them laterally they will quickly begin to turn back to the left. The trick is get them going to the left, laterally, before they turn too much. If you ask how much is too much, you become

Figs. 28A, 28B, 28C, 28D. You can picture to yourself the correlated actions of the hips and shoulders, with the bottom of the imaginary T-square being moved laterally by the hips. This causes the cross-piece of the square (the shoulders) to tip somewhat and bring the hands down inside instead of outside.

hopelessly involved. You might as well ask how many angels can dance on the head of a pin. You don't have to worry about that. Just be sure you get the hips going laterally and that you don't *try* to turn them.

A third reason for the lateral slide of the hips is that this is the movement which *starts the club down toward the ball,* by causing the shoulders to rock slightly as they turn. That movement of the hips—and nothing else—provides the first impetus for the downswing.

It might help you to visualize this action if you think of the spine as being the axis of the swing. Now think of the axis as being a T-square, with the shank as the spine and the crosspiece the shoulders. The end of the shank reaches down to the pelvis or hips. As we address the ball this T-square is, for purposes of the comparison, vertical. On the backswing the hips move slightly to the right, causing the crosspiece to tilt slightly to the left, as it turns, of course, with the turning shoulders. On the downswing (and here is the critical point), the low end of the shank (the hips) is moved sharply to the left. This causes an immediate. and definite tilting of the crosspiece to the right—and that is what starts the shoulders, arms, and club moving down toward the ball. This will be true so long as the whole swinging system is twisted tight, so that a movement against the twist in any one part moves all the other parts. Make no mistake about it, the hips are what move the shoulders and club and start the downswing.

Our second injunction was to *keep the head back.* The head, at this stage, plays a vital role. You have often heard and read that the head is the anchor of the swing. Right here it is. If we keep the head back as we move the hips laterally, it keeps the upper part of our body from going with the hips and thus loosening or relaxing the tension we have been at such pains to build up with the backswing.

This tension that we had at the top of the swing must be kept as long as possible as the swing comes down to the ball. This is one of the chief factors that give power to the swing and speed to the club. If the head comes forward at this point, we lose the tension and get ourselves, in a manner of speaking, "over the ball" as we hit it.

If we keep the head back we do in truth stay back of the ball where we should be. That is what is meant by the advice to "stay back of the ball."

The head, as a matter of fact, has a strange little action

of its own during the first movement of the downswing. Contrary to the old principle that the head must be kept still at all costs, it moves. Pictures of our best modern golfers show that the head not only stays back but that it drops somewhat and, with most, even moves backward a couple of inches.

Almost sacrilegious, this seems. Yet there is a logical reason for it. As the hips move as far as they can to the left, and turn when they can move laterally no farther, and as the shoulders tilt, elevating the left and depressing the right, the body bows out toward the target. If the head doesn't go forward with the body, it has to come down—unless we suddenly grow a few inches during the downswing. An archer's bow may be used as an example of what we mean. The bow may measure five feet from tip to tip before it is strung. When it is strung it curves outward and the distance from tip to tip is less than five feet. When the archer draws it to shoot an arrow, the tip-to-tip distance is still less. When a golfer hits the ball as he should hit it, his body takes the place of the bow: It curves out toward the target and the distance from head to feet is less than when he stands up to the ball.

Another reason the head drops slightly as the ball is hit is that most of the better players develop a rather definite knee bend as they come into the hitting area. They make it a practice to keep both knees bent all through the swing, as they should be, and when they bring the club down to the ball with great speed, the centrifugal force exerted by the flying club head seems almost to pull them down just slightly and hence bend their knees ever so little more.

Our third injunction in this first move from the top was, *Make no effort to move the club.*

The club, of course, will move. It will be moved by the shoulders. What we mean is that no effort should be made with the wrists, hands, or arms to make the club move. That is the important point. If we could turn the arms, hands, and wrists into wood for a fraction of a second as the downswing begins, it would be perfect. Then they and the club would be "frozen" into one solid unit and they would all start down together in one piece, motivated by the rocking, turning shoulders. Then if, with some electronic impulse, we could switch them back to life again as the hands got down to about the hip position, we would have the perfect movement.

The whole downward action is initiated by the lateral movement of the hips to the left. Since at the top we are in a tightly coiled position, this hip action causes the shoulders to rock to the right and turn. The rocking action, with the left shoulder coming up and the right going down, is what moves the arms and the club. If the right shoulder comes down (rocks slightly) as it begins to turn, it brings the upper right arm against the right side and the swing starts down on an inside line. It is when the shoulders turn, throwing the right shoulder high and out toward the ball, that the swing goes outside. Keeping the head back helps the slight rocking action which brings the right shoulder down.

One of the most important things in golf is making this first movement from the top without letting the angle between the shaft and the left arm open. The peculiar thing about it is that if the hip, shoulder, and hand actions are correct, the angle will not open. If they are wrong, it will.

The instant the right shoulder starts to move out high toward the ball, the arm-shaft angle begins to open, even if no

Figs. 29A, 29B, 29C. The eternal triangle. Here we see how the wrist cock is retained through the first part of the downswing, finally breaking open only after the hands get down to waist height or even a little below. Average player, with swing shown in Fig. 26, breaks triangle much too early.

A

effort is made by the hands to swing the club. Most of the time the angle is opened up because the hands are trying to do something with the club. But even without the hands doing anything the angle will still open if the wrong shoulder action is made.

The start down from the top can be visualized in several ways. You can think of it as the "wooden freeze" just mentioned, a momentary period during which nothing happens except what is motivated by the hips.

You can also imagine a triangle, formed on two sides by the shaft of the club and the left arm, with the third side an imaginary line from the club head to the point of the left shoulder. From the top this triangle must be tilted and brought down a ways without changing the length of the imaginary side. This we call the "eternal triangle," because it must be retained as long as possible. As the speed of the club head increases, the imaginary side of the triangle lengthens, of course, and the arm-shaft angle starts to open up. But

B   C

the triangle should be kept constant as long as possible.

We have said several times that the arm-club angle should be held as long as possible. From our use of the words *keep, hold,* and *retain,* you may have gotten the idea that a conscious physical effort must be made to hold this angle. This is not true. What we mean is, if the swing is right, the angle will automatically be preserved until late in the downswing. So, when we say the angle must be held, we mean that you

Figs. 30A, 30B, 30C, 30D. This sequence shows how the left hip and left side lead the hands and the club all the way down and through the ball. It also shows how the hips must go through all the way, to bring the weight far over to the left leg while the head and upper

part of the body stay back. Finally, it reveals how the hips turn toward the target as they reach the extension of their lateral movement. Are your hips ever in this position when you hit the ball?

must work on attaining the correct hip, shoulder, and hand motion which will permit the wrists to remain cocked and the angle preserved. Do nothing, in any event, to get rid of the wrist cock.

The motion is essentially that of the hips. If you have read much about the technique of the swing, you have read that the left hip should lead the downswing. You have read in this chapter that the first movement from the top is a lateral thrust of the hips to the left, eventually followed by an automatic turning of the hips. This is true. But there is more than that (Fig. 30).

The hips must not only move to the left and turn, *their movement must be so closely tied to the left arm that it pulls the arm and the club down and whips them through the ball.*

There must be a definite, conscious feeling that this is happening. It is the single most important movement that a good golfer makes. The effect is shown in Photo C.

This is not to be confused with the mistaken advice to start down with a pull of the left arm. What happens, actually, is that the left arm itself is *being pulled* by the hips. The arm is merely the connecting rod between the hips and the club.

When the hips exert this pulling action, they cause the shoulders and the left arm to revolve so fast around the axis of the upper spine that the hands have little or no time to manipulate or do anything whatever with the club except hang onto it.

If there is one single secret to the golf swing, this is it.

Moving the hips in this fashion would seem a simple thing to do. It is easy to say and easy to understand. Yet nearly all of the vast army of golfers fail to do it. Millions have read it and heard it and seen pictures of it, but just as many millions keep right on starting down with their hands, or pulling with their arms, or stopping the hips after they start them, forgetting to move them all the way through.

They fail for two reasons. The first is that this is a *big* movement and they are afraid to make it. The second is that, preoccupied with what they think they must make the club head do, they completely forget the fundamental hip action and let it die.

The tight connection between the hips and the club, and the consequent pull the club gets from the hip action, is the single greatest source of power in the golf swing. The big muscles of the upper legs and of the torso are giving the club a flying start before the hands do anything.

To visualize what happens it may be helpful to use a mechanical image. Think of a golfer at the top of his backswing. Now imagine a rope, running from the point of his left hip up his left side to his shoulder and then out through his left arm to his left hand. This rope is pulled tight at the top of the swing. As the hips start the downswing by moving to the left and turning, they will pull shoulder, arm, and club with them—so long as the rope is tight.

The rope can be kept tight only if the hips move first and only if they keep moving and then turning, on past the ball. Otherwise the rope will slacken, the pull will stop, and the club never will gain the speed it should reach at the ball. The rope will slacken if, from the top, the shoulders or the hands move first, or if the hips stop moving before they are all the way through.

How do we know when to start the hip movement? We start it the instant we feel the backward momentum of the club start to pull against our hands at the top. This is a reflex action with most of us, but for those who want the moment pinpointed, there it is. And once you start to move the hips, keep them flying—all the way through until they turn toward the target. This action alone will cure a great number of golfing ills.

How It Feels

For you who have been hitting from the top and from the outside for years (and you are about 95 per cent of all golfers), these actions will feel strange indeed, and our problem is how to describe the feeling you should have when you make them.

Words here become of even greater importance than they are customarily. So, since the same action feels different to different people, we will describe several feelings so that perhaps one of them may be recognized.

Once we were giving a lesson to a doctor who was one of the most persistent hitters-from-the-top, outside-in swingers, and hip-stoppers we ever have seen. Telling him to keep his head back, even holding it back for him, failed to give him the idea. Telling him to stay behind the ball had even less effect. Insisting he move his hips through brought no response. Other pros had told him to bring his hands straight down from the top, to bring the butt of the club straight down to the ground, to move his hands toward his right trousers pocket—all the standard gimmicks. He would do these things, in a sense, but he would always manage to turn his shoulders a little first, so when he brought his hands down he brought them down outside.

Finally we said to him: "How do you feel when you are at the top of the swing?"

"When I go there by myself I feel comfortable," he replied, "but when you put me there I am uncomfortable."

That was the clue.

"O.K.," we said. "Just go to the top a few times the way I want you to go, so that you are uncomfortable."

He did.

"Now," we said, "go up the same way, *only stay uncomfortable* as you come down to the ball."

He followed instructions and drilled a 7 iron that was practically perfect—inside out with a late hit. You could see a light go on inside him. The idea of staying uncomfortable as he came down meant, to him, that he had to keep that uncomfortable body twist he had at the top, and the only way he could keep it was to keep his hips moving to the left past the ball. When he started his hips right from the top and kept them moving, he didn't have time to make the little shoulder turn toward the ball that he invariably made to be comfortable, and he didn't have time to do anything with the club head.

Another pupil, who got the idea quicker, said: "My whole idea now is to move my hips so far that I feel them pulling my left arm down toward the ball. When I get that feeling I know I will hit a good shot."

Still a third, an engineer, gave it an excellent expression when he said: "I have the feeling on that first move from the top, when I do nothing with my arms and hands, that I am storing up something—energy or momentum or power—that I am going to release farther down in the swing."

This is a wonderful feeling to have, because that is exactly what you are doing when this first move is made correctly.

You are storing up energy that is going to explode at the ball.

What all this comes down to is two things. First, we coil ourselves up on the backswing to gain tension that is going to be released as late as possible on the downswing. Holding that tension is the "staying uncomfortable" feeling, the "storing up" feeling. That is what gives us distance.

Second, as we move our hips laterally and keep our head back, but *do nothing else,* there is a complete absence of effort in our arms and hands. Then, if we have kept ourselves from uncoiling, the hands and club come down on the inside. That, plus club-face position, gives us direction.

When we have made this first move from the top correctly, where does it bring us? It brings us to a position generally called the hitting area. It is not that, exactly. It is only one position in an infinite number that we pass through in the downswing. It is, roughly, the point in the downswing that we reach before the arm-shaft angle opens up much. The move brings us down so that our hands are nearly opposite our right leg, our weight is over on our left leg, the body is beginning to bow out to the left, the right elbow is nestled against the hip bone, and the club is nearing a horizontal position.

The Check Points

Right here the check points appear. We can't see them in the actual swing, of course, but we can stop the swing now and then and take a look.

If the swing has been made correctly and if the hand-wrist position gained by the backward break has been held, then one knuckle of the left hand should be visible and two of the right, the club face should be at about a 45-degree angle with the ground, the right arm should be firm against the right side, and if the hips have gone through as they should, the player should be able to see the outside of his right leg from the hip to the foot.

Except for seeing the outside of the right leg, these check points are exactly the same as they were after the stationary wrist-break on the backswing.

If two or more knuckles of the left hand can be seen, you have eased up on the wrist position and opened the club face.

A   B

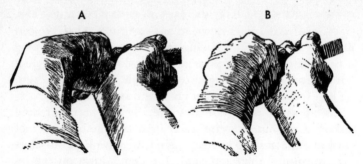

Figs. 31A, 31B. To check your hand-wrist position, stop your down-swing at the so-called hitting position. You should see only one knuckle of the left hand and two knuckles of the right, as in A. If you see two or three knuckles of the left and only one of the right, as in B, you have lost the position gained by the backward break.

If the right arm is not firm against the side, you have turned your shoulders from the top and manipulated the club head. And if you can't see the outside of your right leg all the way down, your hips have not gone through far enough.

So much for the three magic moves from the top. We have seen what they are, how to make them, how they feel, where they bring us, and how to check on them. They probably strike you as strange, and there is no doubt they are elusive, but they are by no means impossible. All our good golfers make them with every shot they hit. Why is it, then, that these moves are so difficult for so many people to get?

Eternal Preoccupation with the Club Head

There are three main reasons. The first is that golfers, like other people, want to be comfortable and don't trust themselves to make a big move. The second is the advice, deep-rooted because it has been repeated for so long, to turn or spin the hips. The third is an overpowering impulse to make the club head move, to do something with it, right from the top. This we call the eternal preoccupation with the club head.

The first and second of these reasons have been thoroughly covered in this and earlier chapters, but the feeling that you have to make the club head do something needs elaboration. It stems, actually, from a complete misunderstanding of the swing, and there are two reasons for the misunderstanding.

The first thing people find hard to believe, apparently, is that a golf ball is driven straight by hitting it from the inside. The average player has the almost overpowering conviction that if he hits the ball from inside this line it will fly far out to the right. He cannot see how anything else can happen. He also knows that when he takes the club to the top of the backswing it is well inside this line. His first instinct, when he starts the club down, is to manipulate the head out onto the line or near it, so he can bring it down along the line and so knock the ball straight.

When the player does this the first movement he makes takes his hands and the club away from his body. The instant they move away they get outside the plane they must be in to hit from the inside.

Before we go further, let's look at the plane of the swing. It is extremely important. If we understand it, learning the right action will be easier.

From the top of the backswing to a point near the end of the follow-through, the head of the club describes what we can call, for convenience, a circle. It isn't a true circle but that isn't important. Suppose we liken this circle to the rim of a wheel. Then we cover the wheel with skin, let's say, so it's like the head of a drum—with a hole in the center for our head to stick through. We now have a flat circular surface, the plane.

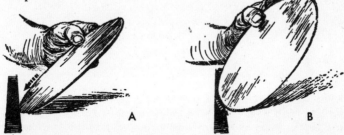

A   B

Figs. 32A, 32B. The plane of the swing represented by a disk. When it is held so that it touches but does not cross the heavy black line in A, it is correct. The club head, following the rim of the disk, would approach the ball from the inside—the inside-out swing. If the disk is twisted a little, as in B, the club head approaches the ball from the outside, the bad way.

During the swing this plane inclines or leans toward the player from 25 to 40 degrees, the exact amount depending

Photo C. Impact. Notice how the hips have gone through and turned, and how much weight has been transferred to the left leg. The hips have led this swing all the way from the top, as they should. Note the distorted shape of the ball at impact. Player is Wes Ellis of the Mountain Ridge Country Club, former winner of the Canadian, Metropolitan, and Texas Open championships.

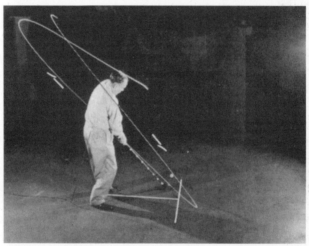

Photo D. The plane of swing in the inside-out swing (above) and the outside-in swing (below). Path of club is traced by electric light on toe of club head. Note position of body, weight on left leg, and head back for inside-out swing; weight on right leg, with shoulders and head turning, in outside-in swing. Player is James J. Dante.

on the length of the club used and on whether the player is an upright or a flat swinger. The bottom of the circular plane touches the line of flight (may cross it slightly) at the ball, then comes back inside and goes on up into the follow through (Fig. 32).

If that plane is twisted just a little (see Photo D), the swing is thrown outside, and you can see how the club head, following the edge of this plane, now approaches the ball from outside the line instead of from inside.

This might make more of an impression if you manipulate the plane yourself. Take a flat dinner plate (preferably not the best china in the house), hold it at an inclination to a straight line on the table. Now twist the plate a little, as shown in Fig. 32B, and see how little alteration it takes to bring the swing to the ball from the outside.

It is just this "little bit" that we have to avoid when we swing a golf club. And when we start from the top to move the club out onto the line of flight with either our hands or our shoulders, we don't change this plane a little bit, we change it a great deal. The result is that we can't help but bring the club in from the outside when we hit.

In this respect it is well to know, too, that at the top a very slight move by the hands forward, or toward the line of flight as they start down, moves the head of the club a comparatively great distance. A mere two inches by the hands moves the club head out a foot, throwing it outside. It is, as we say, already outside as it starts down. When you realize that this slight move of the hands is instinctive—you don't know you make it—then you can understand how hard a pro has to work to cure hitting from the outside.

The Insidious Hand Lag

A second reason for preoccupation with the club head, and this with most people is the chief reason, is the instinctive urge to get the club moving fast. The average player, knowing he must get club head speed to hit the ball as far as he wants to hit it, thinks in terms of the head. It's normal that he should, but that is just another of golf's contradictions. The instant the player tries to move the club head he makes three ruinous actions. He turns his shoulders a little bit, which throws the club outside; he starts to open up the angle between the shaft and the left arm, breaking the eternal triangle; and he stops moving his hips.

Still another thing the average player often does—and this is the most insidious of all—is permit the club head to break the eternal triangle by failing to move his hands fast enough. It is easy to see that once the downswing is begun, the hands and the club must move at the same relative speeds or one will get ahead of the other. The simplest way to alter one of these speeds is to let the hands lag slightly as they come down. When they do that the club head, which is steadily gaining momentum, keeps right on moving, the angle between the shaft and the left arm begins to open, and the imaginary line of the eternal triangle begins to lengthen. You have, in effect, hit from the top and have done it without ever trying to flip the club head or indeed make it do anything. You have just, unconsciously, slowed your hand action a little bit. The triangle has been broken early and the power is gone from the swing.

The reason a great many players make this mistake—and it pursues them all through their golfing lives—is because they subconsciously fear that the club head will never catch up to their hands in time to hit the ball straight. They fear knocking it far out to the right with an open face. So, without ever being conscious of what they are doing, they make sure it will catch up by slowing down their hands, and they succeed, invariably.

This, without a doubt, is the chief reason a practice swing often looks so good and the swing when the ball is there is so bad. In the practice swing there is no fear that the club head won't catch up, so the boys clip the cigar butts and dandelion tops like the pros. They should remember that if the face of the club is square, it makes little difference how far the hands lead the club head at impact.

The attempt to move the club head faster also brings on the hand lag. When a player's efforts are bent on making the club head move, the very effort tends to slow down the hands. Once the hands get behind, they will never catch up; the eternal triangle, once broken open, can never be closed again.

Another peculiar effect of the hand lag is that it tends to prevent the movement of the hips, and the weight, from the right leg to the left. If you will take a few practice swings, deliberately slowing your hands through the first half of the downward arc, you will notice immediately that your weight doesn't flow over to your left side. And as long as you retard your hands, you can't move your weight over.

A pupil came to us recently who said he had been trying for years to move his hips to the left on the downswing but couldn't when the ball was in front of him. His friends had watched him and told him, correctly, that he had no trouble moving his hips on his practice swings. But, once he got a ball in front of him, he could not get those hips over no matter how hard he tried. He was, of course, flat-footed on every ball he hit.

His trouble was obvious after he had hit a few shots. He had the fear of so many that the club wouldn't catch up to his hands at impact, a fear that he would meet the ball with a wide-open face and that the ball would fly out at a wild and dangerous tangent to the right. So, to make certain this catastrophe would not occur, he was slowing down his hands. Once we got his hands moving at the proper speed, his weight moved too. When he found that the club head would catch up after all, his worst troubles were over. Very soon he began to hit the ball more solidly, longer, and with less expenditure of useless effort. When the lesson was over he said he felt ten years younger—and he acted it.

For anyone afflicted with the deadly hand lag there is an exercise that is a great help. We call it the arrested practice swing.

Take a No. 2 or No. 3 wood, tee up a ball, and address it. Now go to the top of the swing and start down at half speed, being sure the hands move with the shoulders and club in the one-piece unit and that the hips move out past the ball. But stop before the club reaches the ball. This swing will retain the wrist cock until the hands are almost opposite the ball.

Done at half speed or even less, the wrist cock can be held until the hands are actually past the ball while the club head is still about six inches or more short of contact.

Make this practice swing four or five times, interrupting it each time before the ball is hit. Speed it up a little but still keep control of the club so that it doesn't hit the ball.

On the next swing, speed it up a little more but don't stop it. Let it go through and hit the ball.

If you are a confirmed hand-lagger, the feeling you will get will be the strangest you have ever felt in golf. You will be amazed at where your hands and hips are, that they can be so far advanced, seemingly far in front of the club head at impact. But that is where they should be, where they have to be if you are to get the late hit and the timing that bring the distance the good players get.

Soon you will get the feeling of bringing the hands down in one piece with the shoulders and the club. You will get the feeling of the hands and the club moving together at their respective speeds through the first big area of the downswing. You will feel that the hands are alive and active, but that *they are moving themselves and are not trying to move anything else.* Those feelings are among the most important in the entire golf swing.

It may help you to visualize the downswing as segments of three circles or rings, one within the other, all connected with each other and all turning. None of these is a true circle, of course, but for purposes of the image let's think they are.

The inner circle is the hips, and the hips move laterally as they turn.

The middle circle is the path taken by the hands as they come down from the top. The outer circle is the path taken by the club head as it comes down.

All three rings are started turning by the first movement of the hips. The club head, assuming a driver is used, starts about three and one-half feet *behind* the hands, owing to the angle of the wrist cock. If the hands are to maintain their three and a half foot lead, they must travel relatively as fast as the club head. If they don't, the club head will begin to overtake them. In other words, the middle ring has to keep moving to keep pace with the outer ring. The instant it doesn't, the outer ring starts to gain on it, the angle of the wrist cock begins to open up, and the swing is ruined.

You may be prompted to ask at this point, how, if the hands must keep their lead, the head of the club eventually catches up (or almost catches up) with the hands at impact. This may be especially puzzling when you think that this happens when the swing is fast but that you can prevent it with the slower one you use in the arrested swing exercise.

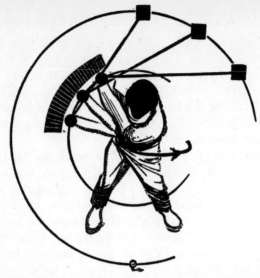

Fig. 33. The three-ring image. The rings are formed by hips, hands, club head. Drawing shows the lead the hands have on the club head at the top and how they must keep that lead as they start the downswing, which is actuated by the hip movement. The shaded area outside the three hand positions is the area of greatest danger. It is here that the hands either try to throw the club head, or lag, waiting for it to catch up.

You are touching now on one of the great mysteries of golf. The answer is in the next chapter. It is enough to say here that it does and always will catch up, due to an immutable law of physics.

Hold the Wrist Position

One more action which must be observed, of course, as the downswing begins, is the retention of the wrist position. You will remember that we started the club back from the ball with an early backward wrist break. This brought us to the top with the right hand under the shaft, the left wrist in a straight line with the back of the left hand, and the face of the club square (at a 45-degree angle with the ground).

It is of vital importance that this wrist position be kept, all through the downswing. This is what brings the face square at impact and gives us a straight shot. If the position is lost, if the left wrist collapses and bends backward, the face opens and the shot is spoiled. So the position must be held, all the way through the ball.

You who have been accustomed for years to having an

open face at the top will feel that you cannot possibly get the ball off the ground with this wrist position. Your feeling will be that the face will be so closed that it will simply bash the ball into the turf.

You are wrong. If the wrist position is held, you will bring the face square to the ball and the ball will fly straight. Many pictures of modern American pros, Palmer and Casper among them, show their club faces almost fully closed at the top. The face points almost straight up.

The reason it is possible to have this position and still hit the ball straight lies in the grip. With the old-fashioned grip, in which three or four knuckles of the left hand were visible at address, such a shut position would bring a bad hook or a smother. The two-knuckle grip will not.

Jimmy Demaret, three times Masters champion, has written: "It is too late to start cocking the wrists at the top of the backswing. The modern method is to cock them at the start of the backswing. The shut-face at the top of the swing (left hand in line with forearm, club face pointing skywards) is gaining in popularity and gives added distance."

There is a strong temptation, though, to relax the wrist and lose the position on the way down. You will not feel yourself lose it, either; it is such an easy, comfortable thing to release.

In this chapter you have learned how and why the fatal flaws develop on the first move down from the top and exactly what they are. You also have been reminded again of the terrible shots they cause. The reminder may have been painful but the gain in knowledge has been great. With it you should be able to replace the wrong moves and faulty positions with the right ones. When you do, you will cut strokes—many of them—from your score.

You have now been through the first three areas of the golf swing, the areas where the fatal flaws develop: the beginning of the backswing, the position at the top, and the first movement of the downswing. There remains only the final phase, the flashing move through the ball. This is intimately connected with the first movement of the downswing, being, indeed, only a continuation of it. Yet it has elements which are distinctly its own, including a highly mysterious action. This will be dealt with next.

7 Through the Ball

Fatal flaw	Club-head obsession.
Awful results	Top, push, dead ball.
Magic moves	Hand-hit out of "eternal triangle," letting COAM take its course.
Check point	A good follow-through.

Once the swing gets down to the so-called hitting area correctly, the chance of its going wrong is very slight. That is because, as we have mentioned, the swing through the ball is only a continuation of the first movement of the downswing, the movement that brings us to the hitting area. By the same token a swing which reaches this area in the wrong position has no chance to get straightened out.

Yet, golf being the strange game that it is, there is still the possibility of the good swing going off the track at this late stage.

In both the good swing and the bad, though, when the flaws appear they appear for basically the same reason— trying to "help" the club head get to the ball.

They will appear in the good swing when the player loosens his left-hand grip slightly and collapses his left elbow. As the result of these actions there comes a peculiar body movement, a sort of heaving action, as though the player were trying, with the body, to help the swing or help hit the ball. It is a very strange contortion indeed. Women, especially, are given to it.

In this movement the loosening left-hand grip and the collapsing left elbow have the effect of bringing the club up sharply instead of letting it go down and through the ball as it should. The left elbow crooks and bends out to the left, toward the target. This suddenly shortens the radius of the swing, and since the straight left arm has been performing the function of a constant radius all through the swing, there is nothing for the club to do but come up.

The horrible result is a badly topped shot. The club, coming up at impact, makes contact on or above the hori-

100

zontal center line of the ball, the ball's "equator." How badly the shot is topped depends only on how much the club is brought up by the elbow action and the shortening of the radius. It is a dead certain way to bounce or dribble your shot into any brook, pond, or ditch that happens to be immediately in front of you.

If the swing happens to be from the inside, the loosening left hand and automatic strengthening of the right hand will cause the ball to be hit out to the right—a push. It may be a topped push or, if the club isn't brought up far enough to make it top the ball, just a push. There is usually trouble to the right on any shot, as every slicer knows, and it doesn't make any difference whether we slice the ball into that trouble or hit a straight ball into it. It still costs strokes.

Fig. 34. The fatal flaw at the ball. Player is so obsessed with moving the club head that he has gotten it ahead of his hands. He has also loosened his grip, bent his left arm, and is "heaving" the club through. A good shot is impossible.

A third possibility these flaws may lead to, if they are slight rather than pronounced, is a straight ball that doesn't go anywhere—a dead ball. This, of course, is caused by the loosening of the left-hand grip. The strong connection between the motive force of the arm and the club that is being motivated is weakened. The connecting link (the hand) gives slightly at impact and force is lost.

We have played with club members who have made this very complaint: "I hit the ball square but it doesn't go anywhere. I must be getting weak."

They are not getting weak. Jim Dent could get the same kind of a shot, relatively, if he loosened his grip as he came into the ball.

The Magic Moves

The magic moves for the good player, of course, are simply to keep his grip tight, hold the wrist position gained by the backward break, *hit through with his hands,* and let COAM take its course. The first insures a strong, live connecting link between the arms and the club at impact. The second insures a square club face. The hard-swinging hands provide the speed. But COAM? What is COAM anyway?

COAM is the Conservation of Angular Momentum. In the golf swing it is the mysterious factor that makes the club head catch up to the hands, *without any effort on the part of the player.* Just a few more paragraphs and we will give you the full explanation.

Fig. 35. The magic move through the ball. The ideal impact position — weight over left leg, head and upper body back, right shoulder coming down and through, left arm fully extended, back of left hand and palm of right moving toward the target. This is the result of all the good moves that have preceded.

For the poor or average player the same magic moves apply, but he must first learn to get himself into the position the good player is in as he reaches the hitting area. He will be in this position if he follows faithfully the instructions in the previous chapter—that is, if, as he starts down, he retains the hand and wrist position, slides his hips laterally to the left, permits no hand lag, and makes no effort to move the club. If he does these things he will keep unchanged the eternal triangle and he will be letting the body move the club. If he doesn't do these things he will never be in the right hitting position. There are just no two ways about it.

Let's take another look at the hitting position, the one the average player finds so difficult to reach (Fig. 36 and Photo A).

Fig. 36. That puzzling "hitting position." Here the player is coming down behind the ball perfectly. His hands have almost reached the ball, but his club head has a full quarter-circle to travel. How does it ever catch up?

The good player has transferred most of his weight to his left leg and his right heel has come up off the ground slightly. His body is beginning to bow out to the left, led by the hips. The upper part of his body, anchored by his head, is still back, and his shoulders have not yet turned past the ball, though the left shoulder has risen and the right shoulder has dropped. His right arm is in close to his body. His hands are near his right leg but the club is still about horizontal and much of the wrist cock has been retained.

The good player here is coming down into a position behind the ball, so that he can hit it "out from under" and from the inside. He is not turning high and over the ball.

The most puzzling part of this picture is the position of the club, or of the hands and the club. The hands are so far down but the club still has so far to go, a full quarter-circle.

Pictures similar to this one have been printed by the thousands since the advent of high-speed photography. They are perfect for showing us how we should be at this late stage of the swing. But we believe also that they have caused more bad shots than any others ever printed.

Why? Because they have implanted—and if not implanted, strengthened—a terrible fear in the mind of the golfer. This is the fear that if he ever gets in this position he will never be able to make the club head catch up to his hands at the ball. Therefore, from this position he feels he would hit worse shots than he hits now, if indeed he were able to hit the ball at all. It looks, to him, impossible.

This is one of the fears that we dwelt on lightly in the preceding chapter—the fear that you will not be able to make the club head move fast enough. It is largely accountable for what we have termed the average golfer's eternal pre-occupation with the club head. He thinks of it as the tool that hits the ball, of course, and right from the top of the swing he starts to manipulate it to make it go faster. Or he retards his hands so the club head will catch up. Even though he knows he should not do these things, his sub-conscious takes command over his reason (as it always will), and he gets an action which has long been known as "hitting too soon," or "hitting from the top," or just plain "flipping."

The deep urge to do this is motivated not alone by the idea that he must make the club head catch up to his hands. Part of it stems from the mistaken idea that he must snap his wrists into the shot. We are not saying this snapping cannot be or isn't done by experts. We are saying that it isn't necessary for the average player. Even worse, it is sui-cidal. The average player, trying to do it, always gets the club head to the ball ahead of his hands.

The frightful result is shown vividly in Photo B. This fellow has succeeded in overcoming all possibility that his club head won't catch up with his hands. It has actually caught them already. It is from two to three feet farther along its orbit than it should be, in relation to his hands. Compare it with Photo A and notice (as soon as you recover from the shock) the differences not only in the club position but in the body, the head, the shoulders, the hips, legs, knees, and feet. The weight hasn't moved to the left as it should, the right foot is flat on the ground, the body shows no bowing-out tendency and the right shoulder is coming around high toward the ball. From this position nothing like the player's potential power is going into the shot. An inordinate part of it has been wasted in making sure the club head would catch up with his hands. A horrible example of what preoccupation with the club head leads to.

This is one of the greatest golf pictures the authors have ever seen for showing how *not* to swing the club. The best part of it, too, is that this is not a posed picture. The subject was hitting a drive during the course of a round and trying to carry a fairway trap about 170 yards from the tee. Funniest part of it is that he *did* carry it. All that proves, however, is how much farther he would have hit the ball (the trap never would have worried him) if he had had even the semblance of a good swing.

The instant you make the club head move faster than it normally is moved by the turning and rocking shoulders, the instant you make it go faster than the hands, the eternal triangle changes shape. One side, the imaginary line between the club head and the point of the left shoulder, begins to lengthen. When this happens early in the downswing, you are lost. The triangle must be kept at the same size, almost down to the hitting area.

When this is done the angle between the left arm and the shaft of the club is retained until the last possible instant and we get what is known as the late hit, which is a sudden catching-up of the club head to the hands as the hands reach the ball.

The opposite of this is the early hit, in which the club catches up to the hands before the hands get near the ball.

In the late hit the triangle is retained through the early stages of the downswing and the player as we noted earlier, experiences the feeling of storing up energy to be released later at the ball. In the early hit he starts moving the club with his hands right away, or he lets his hands lag, and he has no such feeling.

The late hit produces, of course, just what the good player feels it will as he starts down: a high-speed, almost explosive, impact with the ball. The early hit yields only a soft, dying slap. The same amount of energy put into each will bring from 220 to 240 yards with the late hit as against 180 to 190 with the early hit, assuming a driver is used.

COAM—*What It Is and What It Does*

Why is this true? The answer directly involves the hard core of the swing—the physical principle called the Conservation of Angular Momentum, an understanding of which will work wonders for your game.

The golf swing, it should come as no surprise, is a practical application of the science of physics. Physics is the science of the phenomena of inanimate matter involving no chemical change. More simply, it is the study of the strange and seemingly unaccountable things which happen to matter that isn't alive.

One branch of physics is mechanics. A subdivision of mechanics deals with angular momentum, or the rotation of things around an axis.

When an object rotates around a fixed axis it rotates at a constant rate of speed (until friction or gravity slows it down) *so long as the object stays at the same distance from the axis.* If the object is brought closer in to the axis, it automatically speeds up; if it is moved farther out from the axis, it slows down.

Example: a man sits on a rotating stool, holding a weight in each hand. Let him extend his arms to the sides as far as he can, holding the weights at arm's length. Now let someone start him turning. While he is moving, let the man bring the weights in close to his chest. Immediately he will rotate on the stool much faster.

The reverse is also true. If the man starts rotating with the weights against his chest, he will slow himself down when he moves the weights out to arm's length.

A more familiar example is the figure skater executing a pirouette. As he draws his arms in he speeds up his rotation.

The scientist explains this by saying that, if the distribution of mass with respect to the axis is changed, the rotational speeds change.

Remember that the mechanical principle is of the *conservation* of angular momentum. In other words, the momentum, once generated, remains in constant amount, regardless of how it is distributed. In the case of the man revolving on the stool the momentum is distributed back into the man as he brings the weights close to his chest.

The momentum will generally be distributed to the part of the system with the lesser mass, *or* to the part easiest to move. The stool, mounted on ball bearings, was the easiest thing to move in that classic example. But take the case of a man snapping a bullwhip. Here the momentum is distributed from the man's arm and hand and the heavy butt of the whip, into the steadily tapering lash to the light tip. The tip has the least mass and is the easiest thing for it to move. The tip travels so fast—about 840 miles per hour—that it breaks the sound barrier and thus causes the whip to "crack."

Fig. 37. The cracking of a bull whip. The tip moves so fast at the finish, due to the Conservation of Angular Momentum, that it breaks the sound barrier. The same principle causes the club head to catch up with the hands in the golf swing.

Now let's see how COAM applies to the golf swing.

The player and the club may be viewed as a mechanical system. The mass we are interested in consists of the player's shoulders, his arms, and the club. The axis of rotation is a line along the spine, midway between the shoulders.

As the backswing reaches the top, the extensible part of the mass (arms and club) is quite close to the axis. The folded right arm is very close and so is the club, the latter only a few inches distant at that point. The left arm is as close as it ever gets.

Then, when the hips make their lateral movement to the left, turning and tilting the shoulders sharply, the original

Photo E. Conservation of Angular Momentum proved with multiflash photography. Notice how far the cuff on the player's left wrist travels from one flash to the next in area A, and how the cuff images draw closer together, overlapping, in area B (indicating a decline in speed of the hands), just before the club hits the ball. In area B momentum is feeding out of the arms and into the club, causing it to catch up to the hands as they move to a position opposite the ball. Player was one of the game's longest hitters, Jimmy Thomson.

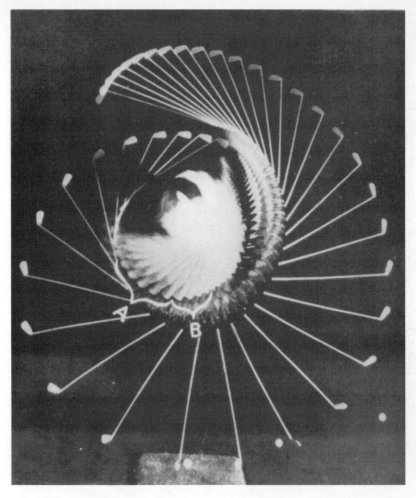

Harold E. Edgerton

Photo F. The same phenomenon revealed with an iron, the hands slowing down in area B as they near the ball, with consequent increase in club-head speed as momentum feeds from one to the other.

momentum is supplied that starts the downswing. The downswing, of course, is the rotational action in which we are interested.

Immediately the arms start down, and as they do they begin to move *away from the axis.*

In the early states of the downswing the original momentum gives the arms and hands considerable speed. As the downswing proceeds, the arms, which are the chief mass, get farther and farther from the axis. The inexorable law of COAM begins to operate and the rotational speed of the arms slows down.

As they slow down—and this is the big point—the momentum generated in the beginning must go somewhere else. It does. *It feeds into the club.*

This increases the speed of the club in the last stages of the downswing, and the club head whips through its last quarter-circle and catches up with the hands at the ball.

We repeat: The club head has to catch up with the hands, *as a matter of mechanical law.* It cannot do anything else.

Yes, we know. You don't believe it. You are jumping up with arguments and objections. Fine.

First, you say, this theory might be logical if we were dealing with an ideal, self-contained mechanical system. But we are not. We are dealing with flesh and blood, with bones, muscles, tendons, joints, and all the wonderfully complex human body. Cold mechanical principles just don't apply.

They don't? The application of mechanical principles has enabled men to jump higher, with and without a pole, to throw a hammer and a discus farther, and put the shot farther. Why should the golf swing be the great exception? The axis is present, through the spinal column between the shoulders, and certainly the rotation is present. Why shouldn't the laws that govern rotation apply, even though the golfer is not the ideal mechanical system? They apply to the man on the stool. It is true that certain of the golfer's muscles do alter the action slightly, but not in the way you might expect. We will explain that later.

If you still think the strength of the hands must be used to bring the club head to the ball on time, try this experiment. Tee up a ball and swing at it with any club you choose. But instead of taking your regular grip, hold the club in only the thumb and second finger of each hand, and as far toward the tips of these digits as possible. Don't have any other fingers touching the club. You may not be able

Figs. 38A, 38B, 38C, 38D. COAM at work. In A, it is generated in the shoulders, where the rotation begins around the axis of the upper spine. In B, it is coming down the arms. In C, it has reached the hands; as they slow down slightly, it feeds into the club. In D, it has reached the club head, giving it the final burst of speed at impact.

to take a full swing but you'll get the club back quite far. You will find that without any effort on your part (it's impossible to apply any effort) the club head will catch up with the hands at impact. The ball will go off the tee, into the air, and straight, if the face is square. It won't go very far, because with that grip you can't swing hard, but it will be a shot. You can do the same thing by swinging with only one hand, either the right or the left. Do you still think you need strong hands and wrists to whip the club head through?

Continuing your objections, you will argue that the arms and hands do not slow down as they approach the ball, that instead they go faster.

The answer is that you *think* they do. Multiflash photography proves that they slow down, in spite of your effort to speed them up. Study Photos E and F. There is less space between the hands down near the point of impact than there is when the hands are in what is designated area A. This means the hands have not moved as far between flashes near the impact point as they moved farther back. They are slowing down, despite the player's effort to make them go faster. As they slowed (because they were getting farther from the axis) the momentum was being fed into the club, and the club head, as the pictures show, was moving faster.

But you still demur. Why, you ask, should momentum feed from the arms into the heavy club? The club is also part of the mass and it, like the arms, is getting farther from the axis. The answer is that the club, although it feels heavy, is actually much the lighter part of the arm-club mass. The club will weigh thirteen to fourteen ounces. The arms of the average man will weigh ten to twelve pounds apiece. The club, then, represents only about 5 per cent of the complete mass.

If you don't think there is enough momentum being fed into the club to make it go so fast near the bottom of the swing, you can do a pretty good job of proving how much there is. Take a club, swing it to the top, and bring it down hard, but try to keep the maximum wrist break you had at the top. Keep it all through the swing. Don't let the angle you had at the top ever open up. Try it. You'll find that it is almost impossible. If, with great muscular strength, you succeed in partly holding that angle, your shoulders will be turned so violently that you will be thrown off balance—off your feet, even, if you swing hard enough.

The reason for this is that when you hold the angle closed, as it was at the top of the swing, you are not allowing much angular momentum to feed into the club, and since you are keeping it from the club, most of it goes into the shoulders.

Now do you believe us when we say that a great deal of momentum feeds into the club when you just let it go?

We think we hear you asking: If the slowing down of the arms causes momentum to flow into the club, why wouldn't it be better to just stop the hands, or try to, at the ball and the let the club head whip through, much as you snap a whip?

The answer is that you can, if you want to, and you won't get too bad a result. The late Abe Mitchell, a fine British professional, did something like that, and he was noted for his long driving. He didn't look good, because he had a peculiar, cramped, choked-off follow-through. Golf writers of the period referred to his influence as "the bane of British golf." What happened, apparently, was that his imitators tied themselves into knots trying to choke off their follow-through, without applying the whiplike lash that Mitchell unconsciously got. It was finally decided that only a man with hands as strong as Abe's could ever duplicate his swing, and the imitators gave up trying.

Actually, a deliberate slowing down of the arms and hands should not be attempted, for two reasons. The first is that it isn't necessary; enough momentum will feed into the club from the hands, and in plenty of time, without trying to force it. The second reason is that the movement of the hands toward and past the ball adds to the speed of the club head at impact. We'll go into this just a little later.

The weight of evidence presented in the foregoing pages should be enough to prove to you that the club will catch up to the hands from the provocative position shown in Fig. 36 and Photo A. That was the first big mystery to be solved.

The second is why the late hit is superior to the early hit, and the third is why hitting from the top so completely ruins the swing. These two have to be considered together, because the early hit is the direct result of hitting from the top and the late hit the consequence of *not* hitting from

Photo B. The wrong hitting position—and how wrong can you get? Compare the position point for point with position in Photo A. The hips are turning somewhat but are not moving laterally. Too much weight is on the right leg, leaving the right foot flat on the ground. The right elbow has not come in against the side. Worst of all, the player has lost all the wrist cock gained at the top of the swing. He has either thrown the club from the top or held back his hands to let the club head catch up. This it has done, although it is still nearly three feet from the ball.

Photo A. The correct hitting position that has puzzled golfers for so long: The hands are almost opposite the right leg. A few more inches will bring them directly opposite the ball, but the club head has a full quarter-circle still to go. How does the club head catch up with the hands? The answer is COAM, the Conservation of Angular Momentum. Note the head back, shoulders rocking, right elbow tucked close in. The player, Joe Dante, is coming down behind the ball with the upper body, but the lower body is moving out to the left ahead of the ball. Hips, moving laterally, are starting to turn as left side gets out of the way, and right heel is rising.

the top.

The explanation goes right back to COAM. Remember the principle, that a change in the distribution of the mass about the axis causes a change in rotational speeds. Now, at the top of the backswing we found that the mass (the club and the arms) was close to the axis. As we start the down-swing with the hip movement we should keep the angle of extreme wrist break that we had at the top. This means re-taining the angle between the left arm and the club shaft. If we do that we keep the club from moving away from the axis quickly and we get a fast rotation. But if we immediately open up that angle we get some of the mass, even though a small amount, moving away from the axis at the *very outset* and the whole rotation is slowed down.

By the time we are halfway down, this retarded rotation, which was never very fast to begin with, has almost permitted the club head to catch up with the hands. When our hands reach the position in Photo B, the club has caught up to them and we get what is called the early hit. In reality it is the slow hit, because the hands never got moving fast enough to make it a fast hit.

Perhaps it will be clearer if you think of it in another way. Take a club and swing it back to the top without any wrist break whatever. It isn't easy, so do it slowly. Now try to swing it down fast, at your normal swinging speed. You'll find you can't do it, at your normal speed. You can't because you can't get it started as fast. And you can't get it started as fast because too much of the mass is too far away from the axis. It's like starting to turn a small wheel and a large wheel of the same mass. It takes more effort to get the big wheel started because the big wheel has most of its mass farther out from the axis.

The correct swing, retaining the wrist break, is like the small wheel. It's easy to get it started and the energy put into it produces a fast rotation. The poor swing, hitting too soon and opening the arm-shaft angle, is like the big wheel, hard to get started and never reaching much rotational speed.

Since the late hit is the fast rotation and the early hit is the slower one, the club head travels faster with the late hit and the ball goes farther.

How the Hands Help

This brings us to something else, the actual function of the hands. Up to now we have regarded them as nothing more than hinges or connecting links between the arms and the club. In a large sense that is true. We never should use the hands to forcibly straighten out the angle between the left arm and the club shaft. We have seen how conservation of momentum does this automatically. But the hands have their use, as does sheer muscular strength, as we shall see.

The original rotational system consists of arms and club swinging around a fixed axis midway between the golfer's shoulders. Now, as the downswing gets under way, the angle between the left arm and the shaft of the club remains (or should remain) what it was at the top. But as the downswing proceeds, this angle begins to open up, slightly. When it does we set up a secondary system of rotation, that of the club alone rotating around an axis formed by the hands. When the hands get down to the hitting position of Photo A the angle opens up very rapidly, as we have seen, until it reaches about 180 degrees (a straight line) at impact.

Within this secondary system there is no added feeding of momentum due to the mass moving farther from the axis; the club is rigid and nothing in it moves in relation to the axis. *But the axis itself moves.* The axis of this system is at the hands, and so it moves along with them in the same direction as the club. They are slowing down, to be sure, because they are getting farther from the primary axis, through the spine, but they are nevertheless moving. Their speed adds somewhat to the speed of the club head. The faster we can make our hands move, down in the hitting area, the faster we will move the club head. This is the point at which sheer muscular strength counts.

At this point COAM is "fighting" the muscular effort to make the hands go faster. Obviously, the stronger the person wielding the club, the greater the force he can apply from outside the system itself—which is what he is doing—and the faster he can make the club head travel.

This, of course, is the point at which the human being swinging the club differs most from the ideal mechanical system on which the principle is based. There are no muscles in a mechanical system.

So the hands do have their part, although the role is not what most of us have thought. Few of us have ever envisioned them as the moving axis of a secondary system of rotation.

Fig. 39. The secondary system of rotation at the hands. The hands are the axis of this system. The faster they can be moved in this area, against the mechanical principal which is slowing them down, the more speed the club will have.

With this new knowledge the deeper mysteries of the golf swing have been solved. We now know why the club head always catches up to the hands at the ball. We know why the late hit is better than the early hit. We know why hitting too soon, or hitting from the top, is so disastrous.

One of the tragedies of golf, if we may be permitted to use a term of that strength in relation to a game, is that men have tried for so long to make the club do what it would do of itself, if merely given a chance. By so trying they have ruined countless swings, tempers, and digestions, and produced untold millions of bad shots.

The Final Proof

This final stage of the swing, as we all know, is a flashing action of such speed that the naked eye cannot hope to follow it. How, then, do we know whether it has been executed correctly or not?

The obvious answer is the flight of the ball. If it goes straight, or if it starts just a little to the right and draws back a little to the middle, if, with a driver, it starts rather low and shows a tendency to climb at a point where the average shot begins to fall, it has been well hit.

The other way to tell whether the right movements have been made, is by the various positions in the follow-through. We have mentioned before that the good follow-through is the result of a good shot, never the cause of it. So, if we have hit the ball with a good swing, the follow-through must also be good. If the swing is bad, the follow-through never will or can be good.

The follow-through is the general position we are pulled into by the great momentum of the club after it has hit the ball. In the good inside-out swing the club tries to go out after the ball but can't because the right hand hangs onto it. So it goes up and around and then down, so that it would be behind the player if he hadn't turned in making the shot.

The player's weight is almost entirely on his left foot, with only the inside edge of the ball of the right foot on the ground. The hips have turned until they are facing the target. The left arm is bent and has collapsed so that the elbow points toward the ground and the left wrist is under the shaft. The right arm, the hand of which has been hanging onto the club, is extended and rather high but not straight, with the back of the hand in line with the forearm. In this and some other respects, the position at this stage of the follow-through is almost exactly the reverse of what it was at the top of the backswing.

If the swing has been from the outside, however, and the player has hit too soon, what follow-through there is will be entirely different. The right heel will be on the ground with much of the weight still on it, the hands will be low and around the body, perhaps even below the shoulders, and the right knee is liable to be poking straight out toward where the ball had been hit. It's a horrible-looking position and it doesn't feel any better than it looks.

These are your check points, and they are strictly effects of the good swing or the bad one. No amount of effort to get a good follow-through, no matter how massive or determined it may be, will ever produce one. It will come only when the swing is good, and then it will come unconsciously.

There are a couple of other checks that the follow-through will reveal. If the swing has been correct, the grip on the club should be just as snug with both hands at the finish as it was at address. You will often find, however, that at the finish the left hand will be loose, that the club has come away from the last three fingers of that hand (Fig. 40B).

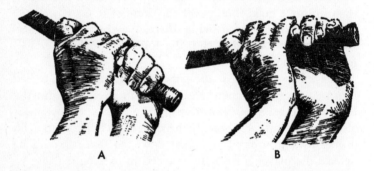

A   B

Figs. 40A, 40B. At the finish of the swing the hands should still be as tight, as in A, as they were at the address. If they loosen, as in B, with the left opening up, certain actions in the swing were wrong.

There are two reasons for this. If the player has "flipped" the club on the downswing, that is, tried to move the head to make it go faster, or if his hands have lagged, the end of the shaft will pull away from the last three fingers of the left hand, and they will be loose at the finish. The other reason is the result of trying to hold the club face square to the line after the ball has been hit, with the mistaken idea of steering it. When this is done the hands do not perform the fast climb-over action that they should, and the end of the shaft literally bounces away from the heel of the left hand. When it does, this hand is loose at the finish.

So if your left-hand grip is not tight at this point, look for one of these two reasons in your swing.

The Strap Treatment

In connection with hitting through the ball, there is a very useful little exercise. It not only gives you the idea of the climb-over of the hands after impact but it helps in other departments too.

We call it the strap treatment. This is not the strap treatment that might be given an erring offspring. It consists merely of swinging, and hitting the ball, with your right arm strapped to your side. A trunk strap is ideal, but a length of clothesline will do. Draw the strap rather tight around your body, enclosing your right arm just above the elbow—leaving the left arm free, of course.

You will find, once strapped, that you cannot take a full swing because your right elbow cannot get away from your body. You will also not be able to get much of a follow-through because the strap will hold your right arm back. Take a few practice swings to get accustomed to the restriction. Then hit some balls.

You will find immediately that in order to get the club back far enough for a decent swing, you will have to turn your shoulders. Next, you will feel that you must hit through the ball hard with your hands. Third, because you cannot let the club head follow out after the ball, the club head

Fig. 41. The strap treatment, a learning aid for confirmed outside-inners and hitters-from-the-top.

will turn over quickly, giving you the climb-over of the hands that always comes with a good shot. And fourth, you will find that if you keep your head back but let your hips slide out to the left past the ball, you will hit from the inside. You cannot do anything else.

The feeling you will get from these four actions can be invaluable. With the strap treatment you are actually swinging in restricted miniature, and the restriction forces you to make and feel correct actions which you might spend months, or even years, trying to learn. The strap is a do-it-yourself gadget of remarkable value.

And now the final stage of the full swing has been completed, its mysteries explained. The mere knowledge of the Conservation of Angular Momentum and the good it will produce, if we only give it a chance, should be a godsend to the struggling player. It should erase the mental block he has had, the feeling that he must make the head of the club move fast, that he must snap his wrists into the shot—many of the very things which have been preventing him from playing better golf.

The long, full shots are not the only ones there are in golf, of course. There are also the little shots, the short game, and the inevitable and highly varied trouble department, all of which we will now proceed to. But these big shots are a tremendous help. If you can hit the ball long and straight, at least half the battle for lower scores is won.

8 *The Short Game*

From thirty yards in to the cup is the decisive area of any golf hole. It is here, most of the time, that the score on the hole is determined. In this area, at point-blank range so to speak, the hole is finished off smartly or it is ruined. Often a bad start from the tee or a poor second shot is atoned for by a brilliant approach and/or a fine putt. More often, unfortunately, the advantages of a good start and adequate play through the fairway go up in smoke because of the approaching or putting, or both. The only time the short game, in one or another of its phases, is not important is when we hit a long shot to within inches of the pin. How often does this happen?

The short game is a forte of the touring pros. Realizing its value, they work on it continually, especially their putting. They use the short game primarily for the birdies they need if they are to win or stay in contention, and, secondly to make up with a par for any errant shot off the tee or through the fairway. The pros need the short game to turn 72's into 66's and 67's, for they will hit from 12 to 17 greens in par figures in the course of a round.

How much more valuable, then, could a good short game be to the average golfer who goes around in from 95 to 105 and hits only two or three greens in par? Think of the shots he could save with a game around the greens that was not brilliant but just reasonably reliable. Imagine how his scores would drop if he could get the ball in the hole in three shots instead of four from twenty or thirty yards, if he frequently took two from the edge instead of three, if he got out of green-side traps in one instead of two or three, and if he holed the two- and three-foot putts he now often misses?

Well, a reliable short game can be developed, though like any other phase of golf it takes work. This, though, calls for technique of a different kind and work of a different kind. It calls for the development of touch, rhythm, and judgment, as distinguished from comparatively big and violent body and arm action to gain club speed and power.

Aggravating as the short game can be when it lets us down,

123

it has two good points. Not much room is required to practice it and no great strength is necessary to become proficient
in it. A man in his sixties, or woman, can develop a
short game as good as the club champion's with work, though
neither could ever get his distance off the tee.

As we see it, the short game falls into four categories: the
short pitch from thirty yards down, the green-side trap shot,
the chip from the fringe, and the putt.

For the average player the primary object of the approach
and the trap shot are to get the ball on the green. Just that
alone. For the better player the object is to get the ball
close enough to the cup to get down with one putt. Yet the
club to be used and the basic manner of playing the shot
are the same for both. The difference in objectives is possible
because the good player has better control through his superior execution and confidence.

The Short Pitch

The average player should play the short pitch with a lofted
club, an 8 or 9 iron, he should aim always for the opening
(assuming there is one), and he should in nearly all cases play
it so that the ball lands on the putting surface, rather than
rolls onto it.

With the 8 or 9 iron the shot is a lofted pitch that will
run a little distance after it hits. The loft of the club will
give it some backspin, if it is struck only well enough to get
it into the air. The spin, plus the fact that it is lofted and so
will descend at a rather sharp angle, will prevent it from
running very far.

If the opening is at the left, let us say, and the pin is on
the right behind a trap, the average player should still hit
for the opening. That is the safe way. The good player will
go for the pin and the chance to get down in one putt.

We advise using the 8 or 9 iron on the shot rather than
the wedge because the average player is more likely to be
familiar with the 8 or 9. The wedge is not the easiest club
in the bag to handle, and this is an important shot that
should be made with the club in which the player has the
most confidence and which he uses oftenest and best.

The shot should be made to hit the putting surface, rather

than the approaches to it, because the ball's action on the putting surface is more dependable. The approach or apron might be rough and the ball could take a kick, right or left. It could be soft or heavy and the ball could stick there. Or it could be harder than the green and the ball could run much father than anticipated. The only time it is advisable to deliberately play to hit short is when the pin is set close to the front edge of a small green.

For the short pitch the stance should be somewhat open and narrower, the heels only a few inches apart. The knees should be bent more than usual with the buttocks in the beginning of a sitting-down position. If a kitchen stool, for instance, were moved in behind the player, he would be just about in position to sit on it. The whole idea of this stance is that we are making a much shorter shot than usual and one calling for more accuracy.

And here, the grip changes slightly too. The right hand remains the same but the left should be turned to the left a little more, so that only one knuckle is visible instead of the customary two, and the left thumb is down the top of the shaft instead of a little across it. This is for accuracy, a brace against turning the hands to the left and pulling the shot. If we slice it a little, it won't matter and besides the ball will come down with more spin on it. But if we pull it, the ball will run and may get us far from the pin. The grip, of course, should be shorter: the hands halfway or more down the gripping area.

Now for the stroke itself. Although a sense of rhythm is important in all shots, it becomes increasingly so the shorter the shot gets. We are down now to a point thirty yards or less from the green, and this shot is almost all rhythm, as distinguished from the wind-up-and-hit shot. By rhythm in this context we mean a deliberate, even, backward-forward swinging of the hands, more like the movement of the pendulum of a clock.

The fatal flaw in the short-game action of the average player is the striking of a quick, hard blow, with the hands stopping and the club head stopping almost as it hits the ball, often digging into the ground. With this kind of stroke, contact with the ball must be extremely accurate and the timing perfect. There is no margin for error. Then, too, we do not want to "sting" the ball, because it leaves the club head fast, and, if struck squarely, is liable to run past the hole. If it is struck the least bit heavily, it pops up and lands short, probably in the trap or the water it was supposed to go over.

A   B

Figs. 42A, 42B. The wrong way to hit the short pitch. Driving the club head at the ball and stopping the hands "stings" it, making it take off lower and run after it hits.

The technique for this short pitch is the same, fundamentally, as for the full shot, except that it is in a modified form. Again we have the backward wrist break; with this short shot it takes the club straight back from the ball. Again the face stays square on the backswing, and again the wrists break early. But the break is not as sharp nor as pronounced as in the big swing. Since the swing is slower the break is slower, and since the swing is much shorter the break never is complete. It is, in short, the same as for the big swing but in miniature—slowed and reduced.

So, in making the stroke, break the wrists as the hands are swung away from the ball, but break them easily and smoothly, with no attempt to break them all the way. Then swing the hands forward and past the ball. They should go

Figs. 43A, 43B. The right way to hit the short pitch of 40 yards or less. The hands go through and the ball rises in a lazy, floating action and drops softly.

through with a slight flex still in the wrists, so that the hands go through the ball slightly ahead of the club head.

Since you are gripping the club down the shaft for this short shot, you will notice that the end of the club will be almost against the left forearm. It should still be there at the end of the stroke. It will be if the hands go through first. If you flick the club and the head goes through first, the end of the club will move away from the forearm. This is an infallible check point.

The club head will take care of itself if we will only let it. The great difficulty with this shot, as well as with the full shots, as we have already said many times, is that we insist on trying to make the club head do something. All that is necessary is to make our *hands* do something.

Since this is largely an arm and hand shot, there is little body movement. Don't try to stop what there is, though, especially whatever there may be in the shoulders.

In this shot, as in the chip from the fringe and the putt,

the thought should always be that the distance is governed by the length of the backswing, never by the amount of force put into the forward swing. And we must always go through this shot with our hands, so that roughly the length of the follow-through and the length of the backswing are the same, with the left wrist still straight at the finish. Never let it collapse.

If you will watch the pros with this in mind, you will see that this is the way they play the shot. We cannot stress too strongly that it should be played this way and no other. It is, again, not the natural way to play it. The natural way is to take the club back a short distance and drive it into the ball, trying to govern the distance of the shot entirely by the force applied. This mistaken tactic, which "stings" the ball, has accounted for more bad short pitches than any other one thing. In the correct shot the ball is not stung. Rather, we should have a mental image of it floating slowly through the air.

The whole swing should be made deliberately, never hurried; but in being deliberate guard against looseness. The two, unfortunately, seem to go together.

A word of warning may be necessary here. The rhythmic shot does not in any sense mean a scooping effort. The ball should be struck just slightly before the bottom of the arc is reached and no effort whatever should be made to lift it. The loft of the club will get the ball up, as it always does if you give it a chance.

Development of the rhythmic type of swing will take some time, especially if you are a confirmed hitter, as most players are. But with practice the feel of it will come. The time you spend on it will be well repaid.

The Chip

The chip shot, by which we mean the run-up played from inches to six feet off the putting surface, can be the greatest stroke-saver in golf. It is here that the good player takes up the slack of an approach that is just a little short, or one that misses to either side by a little, or one which rolls barely over the green. Here is the place the pro or the good amateur shows his class and draws ahead of his high-handicap or only moderately good playing companions.

Take, for instance, a hole measuring 420 yards. This is usually a tough par 4. The 12-handicap player isn't long enough to reach the green in two but he can get there in three, and two putts give him a 5. The pro can usually get home in two easily. But sometimes he will miss the green by a few feet. He then chips close to the hole and drops his putt for a 4. If this goes on for ten holes during a round, the pro could be as much as ten shots ahead even though the 12-handicapper doesn't miss a shot. What it comes down to is that the good players are adept at rolling three shots into two; the poor ones aren't.

How often have you heard a player bemoan his short game? "I had an 84, but five times I took three to get down from the edge." That's the story of many a swollen score by pretty good golfers—three from the edge. Don't think the pros don't lose their touch around the greens too, at times. Then they come in grumbling that their 72 should have been a 69. But by and large the good player's superiority is just as manifest around the greens at it is on the tees.

The mental approach to the chip shot should be to regard it as a short pitch. That's what it is. We employ the same grip, the same general stance, and the same swinging action. The only differences are (1) that the club is gripped shorter, (2) that since we are not going to move the ball as far, the swing is shorter, and (3) that generally a less lofted club should be used.

The grip is taken farther down the shaft for the chip because it brings the hands closer to the club head and thereby gives us better control. Since this is a precision shot, we want all the control we can get.

Although the swing is shorter, the swinging action is exactly the same. With the one-knuckle grip and the thumb down the top of the shaft, the club is taken back in a straight line. The wrists flex slightly. Then the hands go through with the idea of striking the ball with the wrists still flexed.

Again it is exactly the same rhythmic action. As in the short pitch, the distance is determined by the length of the backswing, not by the force of the forward blow. The face is kept square after the ball is hit; the length of the follow-through should be about the same as the length of the backswing. Also, the left arm and the club should form a straight line at the finish, with the end of the shaft in the

A   B   C

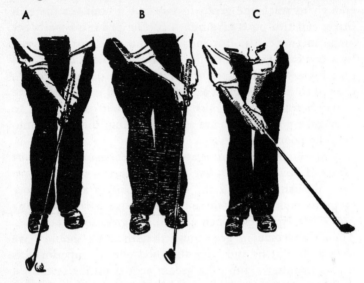

Figs. 44A, 44B, 44C. Technique for the chip shot. With the club held well down on the grip, the end of the shaft extends up behind the left wrist, as the broken lines show. It should still be there at the end of the stroke, as in B. When it is not, as in C, the stroke has been wrong.

same position relative to the left forearm as it was at the address. If the end of the shaft moves away from the wrist, it means we have flicked the club head slightly and *hit with it* instead of swinging our hands through the ball.

The main problem with chip shots, as with putting, is distance, not direction. Most reasonably decent golfers will chip the ball on a good line toward the cup, and we have attempted to reinforce that accuracy by advising that the club be taken straight back from the ball, neither inside nor outside. If your chips are going consistently to the right, it is pretty good evidence that you are taking the club back inside, and if they are going to the left, you are taking the club back outside.

But distance is the problem. There are two ways of gauging distance. One is by picking out a spot on the green on which you want your ball to land, then hitting the ball so it will land there and roll on to die at the cup. This has the advantage of being definite but it implies—nay, demands—an exact knowledge of how far the ball will roll when struck any of varying distances with any club from a wedge to a 4 or 5 iron. This is knowledge, it seems to us, that we might spend a lifetime learning, while we would still make mistakes because of the differences in the lie of the ball and the speed of the green.

The other and sounder method of tackling the distance problem is by instinct. If this seems too haphazard to be dignified by calling it a method, don't be too quick to condemn it.

Archery and golf are a long way apart, it is true, but here is at least one helpful similarity—the problem of overshooting or undershooting. In archery it is called elevation: going too high or too low. Archers attack this in two ways. Some use what is known as a "point of aim." They sight over the tip of the arrow to an object on the ground. Then they shoot and move this object nearer the target or farther from it until they have the exact distance which will, by sighting it, give them the right range.

The other attack is by instinct. By experience, by judgment of distance, by feel—by instinct—they place the arrow accurately without using an artificial point of aim. Naturally, a beginner doesn't have this instinct, but he develops it. And it becomes, with practice, very sharp. It is, in fact, the only way a field archer or a hunter, ever hits anything; if he is hunting bear, for instance, he can't approach the beast and put down a marker to use as a point of aim before he shoots.

A similar sharpness of instinct is developed by golfers. If you were to stand on the fringe of a green and, instead of chipping the ball, you were to pick it up in your hand and roll it toward the cup, you would do pretty well most of the time. Your instinct would dictate how fast you should roll it to make it reach the cup.

"But," you say, "I don't roll it with my hand. I have to strike it with a club."

Our answer is, "Ah, but that is exactly why we have told you to swing through the ball while your wrists are still flexed—so your hands will go through first. It is the speed of *your hands* which determines how far the ball will go. And it is much easier to control and regulate the speed of your hands than it is the speed of the club head. It is easier to *think and feel* how fast your hands are going, because they are a responsive part of you, than it is to think of how fast the head of the club is going."

So, let your instinct govern the speed of your hands, and think only of swinging *with your hands,* not of how fast you should make the club head go. Just as with the big shots, it is our misplaced preoccupation with the club head that gets us into trouble. Don't try to estimate how hard the club head should strike the ball. Instead, let your hands *tell you how fast they should be moved.* When you throw a ball to someone, you do not stop and try to calculate how much effort you should put into the throw to make the ball reach him. You know instinctively; your arm "tells" you. It is exactly the same with the pitch shot and the chip.

What club for the chip? The question has stirred up many a discussion. Some say that the straight-faced irons, even up to the Nos. 3 and 4 should be used. Their argument is that the straighter the face, the less backspin it imparts to the ball, and therefore the distance of the roll is easier to judge. They also say that with the lofted clubs you never can tell exactly how much backspin you will get from one chip to the next, depending on the lie of the ball and the consistency of the green. This group generally visualizes the chip as just a long putt. This is all perfectly logical.

Another group prefers the No. 8 and No. 9, even the wedge. They point out that since these clubs are shorter, with more upright lies, they bring the player (and his hands) nearer the ball, that most players are more familiar with them and that their loft can be easily changed, within limits, by closing or opening the face.

Some claim that the club used should vary all the way from a No. 4 to a No. 9, depending on how long the chip shot is. Others would rather rely on one club for all shots, regardless of the distance.

All of which shows, if nothing else, that there is a difference of opinion about the matter. It is our belief that the Nos. 5, 6, and 7 are the best for chipping in the long run. They have enough loft to raise the ball without trouble, yet not enough to impart the backspin that would seriously affect the running action. There is no reason to doubt tests which have shown that the greatest backspin is applied with a 5 iron. But this occurs when the ball is struck hard, for a full shot. The light impact for the chip imparts little spin.

We would use the 5, 6, and 7 as dictated by the length of the shot being played, and we recommend them as the chipping clubs for the beginner or for the more experienced player who is having trouble with this shot. We believe that the law of averages favors getting more chips closer to the hole with these clubs than with any others. However, if a good player is deadly using a 3 iron for all shots, or using a wedge, we would let him alone. That's the right club for him.

Putting

We have just remarked on the wide difference of opinion concerning the clubs to be used for chipping. That difference is as nothing to those which come up in practically any discussion of putting—from the grip through the stance, the stroke, and the type of weapon itself.

We shall not attempt to go into all these ideas; they could fill a book by themselves. Nor shall we dwell at any great length on the general importance of putting. No one has to be a mental giant to appreciate that one-half the strokes taken in a theoretical par round of 72 are putts—two to a green. Yet 36 putts a round is not considered good putting by any means. This is because no one ever hits eighteen greens in par figures, but instead relies on chipping and short pitch shots to get close enough to get down in one putt on many holes. Hence, the person who cannot consistently hole the short putts and who frequently takes three on a green is in dire trouble. He finds it all but impossible to reduce his score, even though his long game improves.

On the other hand, a good putter with an erratic long game can reduce his score appreciably by straightening out his drives and fairway shots, this with practice and instruction. This fellow will also win a great many matches against players who are longer off the tee and more consistent through the fairway, because of the sheer emotional impact on his opponents of his good putting. There is nothing more shattering to a player's morale than to be on the green in two shots and take three putts, while his opponent is on in three and down in one.

Putting is such an involved part of golf that generalizations are dangerous. For instance, it is easy to say that distance, rather than direction, is the main problem in putting. This certainly is true on long putts. But what about the short putts? From one foot to six feet few of us are going to be bothered by distance. The closer we are to the hole the easier it is to control the distance.

Putting is also such a personalized part of the game that anyone is rash indeed when he becomes dogmatic about method. To any such remark as "You can't do it that way," someone will produce a dozen very fine putters who do it exactly that way. It cannot be said of any really good, consistent putter that his form is wrong. For him it is right. In the philosophical sense, putting form is strictly pragmatic.

Over the long years that a segment of the human race has been "putting little balls into little holes with instruments singularly ill adapted to the purpose," as an Oxford don once put it, there have been changes in styles and techniques. In the late nineteenth and early twentieth centuries, for instance, players in Scotland and England gripped the putter very short. This meant they had to bend over very low. Why this was done we don't know, unless it was to expose less of themselves to the stiff winds of the British Isles.

Through the first three decades of the twentieth century styles were highly individualistic, even among the top players. Bob Jones, for example, stood up quite straight, with his feet practically touching, and gripped the putter at the end of the shaft. During the same period Walter Hagen putted from a decided crouch, with feet spread wide apart. Jim Barnes, a tall, thin man who won both the British and American Open championships, took a very short grip and bent over much more than Hagen, although he was several inches taller. Then there were Horton Smith, Paul Runyan, and Johnny Farrell. Although of decidedly different builds, and using different techniques, all were superb on the greens.

Because of these radical differences, it is often said that great putters are born, not made. There is some truth in this. There are, or surely appear to be, certain individuals with senses of touch, judgment, and control and a general aptitude for getting the ball into the hole which excel those of most mortals. And they do not have to be great or even good players to possess this faculty. Almost every club has one or two of them.

At the same time there is no gainsaying the fact that a poor or very ordinary putter can make himself into a reasonably good one by practice and an appreciation of fundamental principles. It is a fact, for example, that the putting of the American touring pros has greatly improved over the years. Competition on the PGA circuit is so keen, and the standard of play is so high, that those who play the tour consistently simply have to be good putters or quit. Practically all of them are so good, in fact, that it is impossible now to single out any one of them and say, as we could of Smith or Runyan in their day, "He is the best."

Why are so many so good? Because, for one thing, they have given more thought to putting than to any other department of the game. They have theorized more and tested their theories and experiments on such a large scale that out of the great laboratory of the circuit have come certain undeniable truths.

One of these is that putting never can be made a completely "mechanical" action. We put this question to Horton Smith one time, and he, one of the greatest putters of all time, replied at some length:

"No, it never can be entirely mechanical, because we human beings have nerves and emotions. We never will have such complete control of our muscles that we will be able to set the putter in motion and let it make the stroke itself, automatically, so to speak.

"But I do believe that the best putting is a combination of the mechanical and of touch. The closer we can get to the mechanical stroke while still controlling it with our minds and muscles, the better we will be. I know that in my own case it was definitely a combination of the two, working as close as I could get them.

"There have been great putters, a few, who have worked entirely by touch. I've heard that Arnaud Massey, a Frenchman who won the British Open many years ago, was a putter like that. But I've also heard that nobody could possibly duplicate Massey's style."

Probably the nearest approach to the "pure touch" method in the modern era is that of Bobby Locke, the great South African. Locke's putting was as unconventional, by American standards, as were all his other shots. But he had marvelous control of them all and hence was a big winner both here and abroad. But no one ever would attempt to copy Locke's style, either on the green or off the tee. It was too individual.

The thought that Horton Smith expressed has become the keynote of American effort. The goal is to make the stroke as mechanical as possible and at the same time to develop touch and judgment to the highest degree. In pursuing this goal, bizarre, unconventional styles have practically disappeared. Most of the pros today hold the putter at the end of the grip, bend over only enough to bring their eyes directly over the ball, bring the head of the putter straight back, and try to keep its face square to the direction line at all times. Most of them also favor a slightly braced stance, that is, with the weight more on the left leg than on the right. And they favor the reverse overlap grip. They aim to eliminate all movement of both the body and the head and confine movement only to the "working" parts—the arms and hands, some to the hands alone.

All this has brought, in a general sense, a uniformity in putting that did not exist thirty years ago. We no longer see putters with very flat lies (practically all are upright), and we see nothing to approach "Diegeling," the peculiar arms-akimbo position made famous by the late great Leo Diegel, or the one-foot-behind-the-other stance of Eustace Storey, a British amateur. Nor do we see the ample backswing and sweeping stroke of Jones.

Within this uniformity, though, there are differences. The most obvious of these is the way the ball is hit, with either a tap or a stroke, and another is in the use of the wrists, keeping them stiff through the ball or breaking them. Bob Rosburg, 1959 PGA champion, is the most pronounced tapper, his club moving only a few inches back from and past the ball. Sam Snead is decidedly more of a stroker. Art Wall, Jr., was remarkably stiff wristed when he won the Masters in 1959 with five birdies on the last six holes. Few putters broke their wrists more than Bill Casper when he won the American Open the same year, with only 114 putts on the seventy-two greens, 30 under par.

Types of clubs vary much more than styles, although they are of two general types, the blade and the mallet. We are unable to make strong recommendations. Whichever type, regardless of where the shaft is set into the head, feels good to you is the putter for you. Putting is mental and personal to that extent. We do believe, however, that a medium to heavy putter is better than a light one. It is less subject to sensitive nerves and will do more of the work by itself. One further note: If you are putting badly with a mallet, try a blade; you may find it slightly easier to square up with the direction line.

As to the grip, the stance, and the stroke itself, we do have preferences.

Since the grip changes for the type of stroke used, and since we favor a stroking movement rather than the wristy tap, we will give the grip for the stroking movement.

We believe, first, in the reverse overlap, that is, with the thumb and four fingers of the right hand on the club and the forefinger of the left hand overlapping the last two fingers of the right. We like this because the putt is predominantly a right-handed action. We want the right hand in control.

The right hand should be placed on the club so that the palm faces directly to the left and the club is held in the fingers. We are going to move this palm backward and forward and keep it facing directly at our objective. The right thumb lies directly on top of the shaft, pointing straight down.

The position of the left hand is different. It is placed not at the side of the club, not in direct opposition to the right hand, but under the shaft, facing upward at about a 45-degree angle. If you are not accustomed to it, this will feel like a strange position. You simply have to get used to it. The reason for it is that we want to keep the face of the club from opening on the backswing, and the left-hand position under the shaft is the nearest thing there is to insurance that it won't. The left thumb lies down the shaft, a little left of the top.

There are several points in the stance on which there has come to be general, though by no means unanimous, agreement. We should stand with our eyes directly over the ball, the shaft should be exactly perpendicular, the head and body should be completely stationary, the face of the putter should be square to the direction line, and we should strive always for a solid on-the-button contact with the ball.

There are good reasons for all these points. When our eyes are directly over the ball the line to the hole, or that we want the ball to follow, is seen with less perspective than if the eyes are anywhere else. The shaft should be perpendicular because when it is, we are much more likely to strike the ball exactly at the bottom of the swing arc. Any movement of the head or the body is liable to move the hands and throw the ball off line. The head can move three or four inches on big shots but one inch can ruin a putt. If the face of the putter is not square to start with, we certainly will have a harder time bringing it square at contact. The flush, solid contact should seemingly be easy with a putter, yet how often have you hit a putt and gotten a dead, off-center feeling? Some putts hit off center will go into the hole, no question about that, but those which are hit flush are much more likely to drop. A putt hit off center is an indication that something has gone wrong with the stroke.

Opinions on other points of the stance differ, but we prefer a slight spread of the feet, so that more weight can be placed on the left leg, giving us a braced feeling and less likelihood of body movement.

We also want a square stance—the points of the toes an equal distance from the direction line. This makes lining up the putt easier.

The ball itself should be played opposite the left heel or a shade inside it. We realize this is at variance with the practice of many good putters who play the ball opposite the left toe. We feel that with the heel position there is less chance of pulling the putt. If it is played farther back there would be a tendency to push it.

The stroked putt itself is almost a chip shot in miniature. The club is taken straight back from the ball with the arms, the arms hinging at the shoulder joints, and the face kept square. At the end of the backstroke there is a slight, backward break in the wrists. The hands and arms are then moved straight to the left, and the head of the putter is taken through the ball with no break whatever in the left wrist. The right hand is in command at all times and on the forward stroke the palm of this hand should be moved straight at the objective.

We believe, along with many others, that the ball should be struck exactly at the bottom of the swing arc. We see no point in hitting it on the downstroke or the upstroke. These merely complicate the putt, an operation most players find difficult enough at its simplest.

The rhythm of the stroke should always be the same, with the length of the putt determined by the length of the backswing.

All of this constitutes the stiff-wristed stroke, the method most players will find easier to learn and to execute than any other.

The wristy tap is entirely different. In this, since all movement is confined to the hands and there is no hinging at the shoulders, the hands must be exactly opposed in the grip. The left cannot be under the shaft but must exactly face the right.

In the stroke itself the arms do not move. The hands simply bend backward and forward at the wrist joints. Because the arms don't move, the head of the putter is brought up higher on the backstroke and higher again after the ball is hit on the forward stroke. And here there is more of a feeling that the putter is pushed back by the left hand and brought forward with the right.

Pros on the circuit appear to change from time to time, many of them combining some elements of each style. Cary Middlecoff, at his peak, was perhaps the best example of the compromise between the two. Middlecoff appeared to stroke the ball yet at the same time to give it a right-hand tap. Some pros also feel that the wristy tap may be better for the long putts but prefer the stroke for the shorter ones, on the theory that the wrists, being sensitive, are more liable to be affected by jumpy nerves than are the arms. It is largely a matter of which style works better for the individual doing the putting.

One thing which you should do in putting is develop a

140

A

Figs. 45A, 45B, 45C. Arm putting. The arms swing from the shoulders. The putter is taken through the ball with no break in the left wrist.

B

C

definite pattern of movement, a sort of time-motion formula, in which the same motions are made each time, and the same amount of time is consumed before the putt is struck. Julius Boros, a big and consistent money winner among the American pros, exemplifies this to a marked degree. Boros sizes up the putt thoroughly before he takes his stance, but once he gets over the ball there is no hesitation. His first movement then is to place the head of the club in front of the ball, his second is to place it behind the ball, his third is to start the stroke. The pattern never varies, regardless of the difficulty or importance of the putt.

A friend once mused, "I wonder if Boros ever lies awake nights wondering how many more he would have holed if he'd taken a little more time."

A fellow pro answered with, "I'm sure he doesn't. He's found that this pattern works for him. He may occasionally miss a putt that he'd have dropped if he'd taken more time, but there are more that he makes that he would have missed if he'd hung over the ball, agonizing."

That is what we mean by a pattern, a time-motion formula. Your pattern is not likely to be the same as Boros', but develop one and then stick to it. In the long run you'll find it saves you strokes.

Another thing which should be borne in mind about putting: Don't clutter your thinking with ideas about applying overspin, sidespin, or backspin to the ball. You can't do it. Alastair Cochran, an English physicist, recently demonstrated that any spin which happens to be applied disappears long before it reaches the hole. The idea that overspin can be put on a ball which will make it dive into the cup is the rankest fallacy.

All putts skid slightly before settling into a true roll. The harder the ball is struck, the more it skids. A ball struck with a slightly descending blow will skid more than one struck with a perfectly horizontal blow. A putt that is partly topped will skid less than either, but who wants to go around trying to partly top all his putts? Nor does it make any difference whether you tap the ball or use a sweeping stroke, so far as the mechanical action of the ball is concerned.

No, your concern in putting should be only to meet the ball squarely, with the club face facing exactly in the direction you want the ball to start moving.

The one indispensable ingredient in this department is confidence; not confidence that you will sink every putt regardless of its distance, but confidence that you will be able to handle, with the method you use, any putting situation that may arise.

The Green-side Trap

All trap play, we suppose, should be classed as trouble and treated in the chapter devoted to trouble. Bunker shots certainly cannot be identified as one of the pleasant interludes in a round of golf. Yet traps around the green are in the scoring area, hence they fall into the category of the short game. When we speak, for instance, of Boros, 1952 American Open champion, as having a great short game we don't think only of his putting, his chipping, and his short pitches. We also think of his trap play around the greens. Exactly the same is true of Casper, the 1959 champion, and others whose short games are unusually good. Their recoveries from sand are integral parts of their games in the scoring zone. Time after time they come out close enough to get down in one putt and avert a penalty they invited.

We don't have to tell you much about the traps themselves. They vary widely: some deep, some shallow, some with fine, fluffy sand, some with coarse, heavy sand. And you likewise know that the lies you can get in traps can run all the way

A

Figs. 46A, 46B, 46C. Wrist putting. The arms remain stationary, the hands breaking backward and forward at the wrists.

from clean to embedded. One lie you don't get much today is one in the bottom of a heel print. Many courses now have rakes at each green and a caddy smoothes out the footprints, even if the player himself doesn't.

We will consider first the clean lie, with a bank of no more than three or four feet to clear.

The first task is to get the ball out of the trap and on the green. Never mind, yet, about getting close to the cup. From anywhere on the green you have at least a chance, even if the ball is sixty feet away, of holing the putt. But if you leave the ball in the trap with your shot, you have practically no chance. Never forget that.

Let's consider the special club used for the last thirty years, approximately, for getting out of the sand—the sand wedge. This club has made the job much easier than in the days when a niblick, to which our No. 9 iron corresponds, was the tool.

The niblick, at least prior to 1930, was a comparatively thin-bladed club with a deep face. The tendency in hitting an explosion shot with it was to dig too deep and leave the ball still in the sand. Because of this the so-called half-blast was developed. In this the player took a very open stance, laid back the face, and tried to take just a thin layer of

B

C

D

sand under the ball with an out-to-in swing. If this shot was mastered it had two good points. It lessened the likelihood of digging too deep, and it imparted a great deal of backspin to the ball. Such a shot was aimed a little to the left of the pin, because when the ball hit the green with the backspin applied from the outside, it would draw up and kick to the right. Such a shot was fine, if the execution was good; the trouble lay in mastering the execution. A little too much sand and the ball stayed in the trap. Not enough sand and the player was likely to decapitate anybody standing on the opposite side of the green.

Then came the sand wedge. This club differed from the niblick in being heavier and, more importantly, in being very thick about the sole, which was flanged. The flange had —and still has—the effect of a plane, which tends to keep the club head from digging too deeply into the sand. It rides through it more or less horizontally. The wedge is not foolproof by any means, as millions of golfers have found out; but it is a better club, a more reliable tool, than anything else produced and permitted by the United States Golf Association. Now let's see how this tool should be used.

The first thing to do, as you take your stance, is shuffle your feet down into the sand until they have a firm base. There are two good reasons for this. The first is to give you the firm base, so that during the action of the swing, as the weight shifts, one foot won't sink farther down than at the beginning of the swing. Such a drop, if it is only an inch, can spoil the shot by lowering the arc of the swing and causing you to take too much sand. The second reason for the foot-shuffling is to give you an idea of the texture of the sand and how much of it there actually is in the area of the ball. You may find there is very little, or that it is hard or deep or fluffy, as the case may be. Since the rules prevent you from touching the sand with your hand or the club, give your feet a chance to tell you.

The next thing to bear in mind about the wedge is that it is heavier than your other clubs and therefore is able to do more work by itself. In other words, it doesn't have to be swung so hard, for the shot of average length. Of far more importance than any application of power is the necessity for accurate contact with the sand. Once the club is started moving, if the hands are kept moving through the ball, just as in any other type of shot, the club will go through without any extra burst of speed or power. Rare is the average player, though, who doesn't give it that extra burst, because he fears the club will stick in the sand and the ball will stay in the trap.

This brings us directly to the second point, which is the importance of hitting the sand where we aim to hit it. Since the whole idea of the explosion type of sand shot is to swing the club through the sand under the ball, with the ball thrown up by the sudden upward displacement of sand, the amount of sand thrown up is the determining factor. The amount thrown up is determined by the distance behind the ball that the club enters the sand and on how steep the downward path of the club is. The steeper the path, the deeper the club will go in spite of the flange on its sole, and the greater will be the amount of sand displaced. If there is too much, the ball won't be raised enough to get it out of the trap. If there is too little, the ball will come out too far and probably go right over the green into a trap on the other side.

The ideal point to strike the sand is two inches behind the rear face of the ball, with a swing more upright than the one taught for the other shots.

As you start to address your ball, then, the first thing to do is pick out a spot in the sand that you estimate is two inches behind it. This is just about the distance from the tip of your index finger to the second joint. There is always some good little target to aim at: a pebble, a black speck, a white speck, something. The idea is to have the sole of the club enter the sand at this point. You should always remember that you will be much more accurate in hitting the spot if you swing easily and rhythmically and let the club do the work.

As for the shot itself, the stance should be moderately open, the feet rather close together, as for the short pitch, the grip the same as for the short pitch (one knuckle visible), and the ball played about opposite the left heel. The face of the club should be opened just a little (Fig. 47).

The swing itself should be made with the same early backward wrist break as for a full shot, but the swing should not be full. It should be about a three-quarter swing and slightly more upright than normal. Most of the weight should be kept on the left foot throughout. This is to promote a more accurate contact with the sand and to avoid a possible shifting of stance (Fig. 48).

Fig. 47. The explosion shot. The stance, with the explosion idea superimposed. Stance is slightly open, so is the club face. The idea is to drive the lofted wedge into the sand behind the ball, exploding sand and ball upward.

With a three-quarter swing the wrist break will be complete, for the hands will be more than hip high. From the top there is the same hip and shoulder action that there is for the full shot, except that it is less violent. The effort should be about what it is for a fifty-yard pitch shot. As in the other shots the hands should tend to go through the ball ahead of the club head, with determination but not with great speed. The hips should lead, with the upper part of the body staying back, just as in a full shot.

A difference you may notice at the finish is that the club will not come up far out of the sand. Its momentum has been spent going through it. For this reason the right hand does not climb over the left. None of this matters though, for by that time the ball is out of the trap and safely on the green—we hope.

This is the shot to be used from a clean or nearly clean lie, in dry, loose sand. The distance you want the ball to travel

Fig. 48. Top of the swing for the explosion. Notice that the swing is more upright, shorter, and with less break in the wrists than for an ordinary pitch. Also, the face of the club is open.

is determined by the strength of the swing, not, as in the other shots, by the length of the backswing. In sand, keep the length of the swing the same for practically all shots, but vary the amount of effort depending on the distance to be covered.

If the sand is wet or packed hard, take less sand by hitting closer to the ball, keeping the length and strength of the swing the same.

For an embedded lie, where three quarters or all of the ball is below the surrounding surface of the sand, a different technique is called for. For this we play the ball back farther, almost back to the right foot, open the stance less or not at all, close or even hood the face of the club, and hit down hard, close behind the ball (Fig. 49).

The idea here is to get the club down into the sand to raise the ball and at the same time to get it moving forward toward the target. Playing the ball farther back and closing the face of the club accomplishes both objectives: The club digs deeper and the lessened loft of the club face propels the ball forward.

For this shot we still prefer the sand wedge, although some players will use the pitching wedge for it and even the 9 iron. The reason for selecting the other clubs is that the pitching wedge has less flange on the sole than the sand wedge and the 9 iron less than the pitching wedge. These clubs, therefore, will cut down into the sand more easily.

Fig. 49. The embedded lie can be handled. Notice that the ball is played back toward the right foot, that the hands are ahead of it, that the stroke will be more sharply descending, and that the club face is closed. All this imparts more of a forward, less of a lifting, motion to the ball.

Occasionally you will find yourself in a trap with its almost perpendicular face directly in front of your ball. If you are to get out toward the hole, you have to get the ball up very quickly. This is done by opening the stance more and opening the face of the club more. The more the face is open, the more force will be directed upward on the ball, and the less force forward. Unless the ball is embedded or in a bad lie, it will come up quickly enough to clear the face of the bunker.

These are the shots, then—the short pitch, the chip, the putt, the green-side trap—that take up the slack when the long game falters. These are the ones that help us atone for mistakes, that give us a second chance when the long iron strays or the full pitch doesn't quite have the legs. They get us the pars when the bogeys stare us in the face. And the putts, when our long game is on the beam, get us the birdies.

So seize every chance you can to practice the short game. It's the easy department of golf to work at, and it pays tremendous dividends.

9 *In and Out of Trouble*

On a golf course, as a rule, trouble comes at us swiftly and unexpectedly. There are times when we do not quite expect to carry a brook or a cross trap, or when we know we can easily miss a green with a wood or a long iron. Then we are not surprised when we find ourselves in difficulties. But much more often we stand on a tee, with a wide fairway beckoning, swing—and find ourselves in the woods or heavy rough.

Generally, there are three kinds of trouble we can reach with a shot off the fairway: woods, rough, or a fairway trap. The first thought in each case should be to get out of the trouble, whatever it is. Good players have often made great shots from seemingly impossible positions. That's fine, for them. But not for you.

Woods and Rough

In the woods, unless you are extremely deep, there is an opening of some sort. Play out through it, even if you have to play the shot back toward the tee. But get out on the fairway. If, by any chance, you are going to make a great shot, the fairway is the place to do it, not the woods. Any club that will get you out safely is the club to use.

From the rough, much depends on the distance you can safely try for and still get the ball into the fairway. Rough is of almost an infinite variety, from thin, short, scraggly grass, which often gives you a lie no worse than one in the fairway, through short, dense, clinging grass to high grass and weeds.

There is probably no rough so thick that a ball cannot be extricated from it and delivered a short distance with a sand wedge. The trouble with us is that we try to get real distance from the rough and often wind up with the ball advanced only a few yards and still in the long grass.

In making almost any shot from long or heavy grass, the point to remember is that we must hit down on the ball with a club lofted enough to be sure we get the ball out, regardless of distance. To get a sharp downward stroke we will make it easy for ourselves if we play the ball back to a point midway between our feet and, if the grass is at all heavy, take a slightly more upright swing.

It is impossible to give any rules as to what club should be used. That depends entirely on the texture and height of the grass, the lie of the ball, and the distance you think you can get while still, with safety, getting clear of the rough.

You should remember, though, that if an iron is used the ball will come out with less backspin on it—even none at all —and therefore will run farther than you expect. This is because the grass, getting between the ball and the face of the club, reduces the club's "grip," the normal friction between ball and club face. A shot from the rough is less likely to hold a green but it will pick up distance on a fairway.

It is also worth mentioning that surprising success is quite often possible with a No. 4 wood, if the lie is not bad. The more rounded head of the wooden club slips through the grass more easily than the barlike head of an iron. The latter catches a lot of grass, slowing the speed and cushioning the blow. That is why, with the irons, we strike a more sharply descending blow in the rough, to get as little grass as possible between the club face and the ball.

Fairway Traps

The traps placed to catch errant drives, or wandering second shots on par-5 holes, are usually shallow. If they are not, waste no time thinking about how to get distance from them. Just get out on the fairway with whatever club will get you there.

But when they are shallow, it is possible to get quite a bit of distance from them if the lie is good. Let whatever distance you try to get, though, be dependent entirely on a club that will get you safely out. For instance, from a good lie you might be tempted to use a 4 iron. Don't be tempted. Use a 5 iron and be sure.

For the shot itself the feet must be wriggled into the sand as in the green-side trap, for a firm, no-slip base. The grip should be shortened and the swing shortened. The ball should be played no farther forward than midway between the feet, usually a little back of center, and the weight should be kept on the left leg. Then the shot should be hit as from the fairway but with the shortened swing.

By way of explanation, we want the grip shortened because the feet, after you shuffle them down, are lower than the ball. The swing should be shortened for control, to produce a more accurate contact between club and ball, for accurate contact in sand is of vital importance. The weight on the left leg helps to insure that we will not hit the sand first, an act that is certain to kill the shot. If that happens, the ball will go only a few yards and may not even get out of the trap. Theoretically, the ball should be hit at the exact bottom of the arc of the swing, but it is far better to hit the ball first than to hit the sand first.

Obstructions

Most obstructions on golf courses are trees, though there can also be mounds, bushes, hedges, fences, and occasionally a shack. Most of these offer little problem. Even the trees, sometimes, are no problem either. If your ball is so close to a big trunk that you can't get around it or can't swing the club, there is no alternative; you just have to waste a shot by hitting sideways out to the fairway, trading a stroke for position.

Usually, though, something can be done with a tree. You can go over it, or under it, or around it to the right or left. What you do depends on the size of the tree, how low its branches are, how far your ball lies from it, and how far it is from the green.

To do all these things requires the ability to get the ball up quickly, to keep it low, to hook it, and to slice it.

If the ball must be gotten high quickly to get over a small tree, for example, the safest club is the pitching wedge. Its face should be opened slightly, and the ball should be played a little farther forward than usual and hit down on with a full follow-through.

Conversely, if the ball must be kept low, perhaps to go under the branches of a big tree, the opposite technique is employed. A club with a straighter face than the distance the shot calls for should be used. The ball should be played midway between the feet or farther back, the club should be toed in slightly, the weight should be kept on the left leg, and a shorter, stiffer-wristed swing should be used with a very short follow-through.

The intentional hook and slice are more difficult, despite the fact that the slice should be easy for the average player. The strange thing is that when such a player *tries* to slice he often hits the ball straight.

Of the two shots, however, the slice is much the easier. To produce it with the normal swing, the ball should be played a little farther forward, the stance should be opened slightly, both hands should be placed a little more to the left in the grip (the left more to the side, the right more on top), the face should be opened slightly, and the swing itself can be a shade more upright. An effort should be made, in slicing, to keep the face of the club square after the ball is hit; in other words, keep the right hand from climbing over the left as long as possible. All this should impart a left-to-right spin and cause the ball to curve to the right.

For the hook, the positions and actions are exactly reversed. The ball is played a little farther back than normally, the stance is closed, both hands are placed more to the right on the shaft, the face should be closed slightly, and the swing should be flattened unless it is already a flat swing. In going through the ball, no attempt should be made to keep the face square after impact; if anything, the turning-over action of the hands should be slightly emphasized. This should put the desired right-to-left spin on the ball, resulting in a hook.

Lies of All Kinds

Few things annoy the average golfer in an ordinary round more than an uneven lie in the fairway. For this fellow, getting the ball in the fairway at all is often quite a feat. When he succeeds and then finds he has to hit his second shot from an uphill, downhill, or sidehill lie, he is likely to feel that the gods are against him.

Most uneven lies do complicate the shot, for they call for techniques that aren't quite normal, and heaven knows the average player has trouble enough executing the simplest routines.

They are not all bad, though. The straight uphill lie, where the player's left foot is higher than his right, is not a hard shot to hit. Neither is the sidehill, where the ball is only a few inches higher than the feet. In fact, there are many players who hit this shot better than those from level lies.

The only difficulty with the uphill lie is in getting the weight transferred over to the left leg as we come into the ball. We start the swing with most of our weight on the right leg, due purely to the pull of gravity, and it will stay there unless we make a strong effort to get it over to the left.

The tendency on this shot is to take a big, full swing. Don't do it. Take a shorter grip, a shorter backswing, and pivot less. It will be easier to keep your balance and control your weight. Also, use an iron (if you are using an iron) one club stronger than you would if the shot were from a level lie. The slope of the ground increases the loft of the club, and you may find yourself short unless you use the stronger iron.

This shot should be played a little to the right of the target because of the tendency to pull or hook from an uphill lie. This exists because the weight doesn't get over to the left quickly enough.

The mental attitude toward the uphill lie is generally good, and this helps. The player feels he will have no trouble getting the ball up, and since that is one of his major problems from a level lie, he has one less worry when he hits the ball uphill.

The downhill lie is just the reverse, of course. Here he feels he can't get the ball up, and often he is right. The trick is to stay down to the shot all the way through. The ball should be played back a little farther between the feet, a club with one number more loft than normal should be used, and, as with the uphill lie, a shorter grip and shorter swing should be employed for control. This shot is likely to drift to the right, so allow for it by aiming a little to the left. But by all means stay down to the ball, and make the head of the club follow low along the slope of the ground.

There is one factor in playing a shot from a downhill lie that actually helps the average player, though he seldom realizes it. Getting his weight over to his left leg quickly on the downswing is easier than from any other lie. Gravity, in this case, helps him get into the right position. If he will remember this, his attitude toward the downhill lie will be greatly improved.

The sidehill lie, when we are standing a few inches below the ball, is not a hard one. We need only to play the ball back a little, grip shorter, and play for a slight hook. It will also help, perhaps, if we stand up a little straighter and open the stance slightly. The shorter grip and the more upright stance will be almost instinctive, for we are actually nearer the ball than if we had a level lie.

The sidehill lie in which we are standing above the ball is the real villain, causing more bad shots than any other uneven situation. The big trouble here is in getting down to the ball and staying there throughout the swing. We have to grip the club long for this one, bend our knees more, hunch over more, play the ball back farther, and it will be well to toe in the club slightly. Here also we should definitely take a shorter, more controlled swing and be certain to stay bent down to the shot until the ball is well on its way. We are very apt to slice from this position, so it is best to play the ball somewhat to the left of the target.

Other difficult lies we get in the fairway are in divot holes once in a while, from bare ground occasionally, and, more often, from heavy or clover lies.

In a divot hole, if we play the ball back a little, keep the weight to the left, and try to drive the ball deeper into the hole, we should have no trouble.

From bare ground we should close the face of the club slightly, make sure to keep our hands ahead as we go through, and pinch the ball, making certain we hit it before we do the ground.

A very heavy fairway lie should get the same technique we use from the rough. That is, play the ball back somewhat, hit down on it with a more upright swing, with a club one number more lofted than the shot seems to call for. As with a shot from the rough, the ball will run, because, even though we try to get as little grass as possible between ball and club at impact, we are sure to get some and backspin will be slight.

Just an elementary knowledge of how to handle all these fairway lies should help the average player. There should no longer be a feeling of utter helplessness. We are now armed with techniques which will enable us to meet the situations halfway, at least.

10 *The Early Break and the Late Hit — Secrets of Timing and Rhythm*

Whenever we go to a golf tournament and see a really good player hit the ball, we receive two vivid impressions. The first is how far the ball goes with seemingly so little effort. The second is of a certain measured cadence in the upward and downward movement of the club. Both are accurate impressions.

Now if we happen to be on the practice tee, where we can watch this player hit shot after shot, we will notice two other things. One is that he swings all his clubs at about the same speed; he doesn't seem to hit the 3 wood any harder than he hits the 7 iron. The second thing we notice, when we let our gaze wander to other players practicing, is that while most of them are deliberate, there are differences in their swinging speeds.

Timing is the answer to the first accomplishment—the long hit with little effort. *Rhythm* produces the measured cadence in the upward and downward movement of the club. And the differences we notice in swinging speed among other players are differences in *tempo*.

Nearly all good players will give us impressions of timing and rhythm. The more graceful the player, the more vivid the impression will be. Sam Snead, among the moderns, is the perfect example. Among the giants of the past, Bob Jones's swing was once called the "poetry of motion," and the late Macdonald Smith was probably the most effortless swinger who ever played the game. The players of today swing harder at the ball than did their predecessors, with the result that theirs is more of a hitting than a swinging action.

Yet the ball still flies out much farther than it should, for the effort the player seems to be putting into it. This is very marked in the graceful players of smaller stature, such as Gene Littler, 1961 National Open champion, and Dow Finsterwald, former National PGA champion.

156

Timing

The answer to the effort-distance puzzle being timing, just what is timing? For one thing, it is a word that has been used more loosely, perhaps, than any other in golf literature. We have been blandly told that we should work to improve our timing, that our timing is off, that without good timing we cannot hope to play well. But there, having given the word the once-over-lightly treatment, the oracles have left us. They have never adequately explained timing or told us what we should do to improve ours. Our private guess is that they don't know themselves what it is.

A dictionary will tell you that timing is: *"The regulating of the speed of a motion, stroke, or blow, so that it reaches its maximum at the correct moment."* In golf, obviously, this would mean regulating the speed of the club head so as to cause it to reach its maximum as it hits the ball.

The key phrase is "regulating of the speed." The better the speed is regulated, the better the timing; the poorer the regulation, the poorer the timing. It is here that at·least 95 per cent of all golfers have their worst trouble.

They have it because the regulation of the speed depends not on how the club head is manipulated by the hands but on how and when other parts of the swinging system operate: the hips, the shoulders, the arms, the hands. If these move in the right way and in the right order, they will automatically regulate the speed of the club head so that it reaches its maximum as it hits the ball. It is, in effect, a chain reaction of movement, with the club head getting the final effect.

The reason the vast majority of golfers have such trouble timing a shot satisfactorily is that, subconsciously or consciously, they try to regulate the speed of the club head *directly* with their hands, without using the intermediary links of the hips, shoulders, and arms. When they do this they get an early but never very great reaction, in terms of speed, from the club head. This is the old familiar "hitting too soon" or "hitting from the top." When the intermediary links are used and the chain reaction is allowed to take its course, there is a late reaction by the club head, which then accelerates to great speed at impact. There is a common expression to describe the player who uses the chain reaction: "He waits on the club." It may not be grammatical but it is descriptive.

What this all comes down to is, the expression of good timing is the late hit. The expression of poor timing is the early hit. We have already, in previous chapters, explained the moves that produce the late hit and the early hit. Here, as we discuss timing, we isolate one key move that leads to good or improved timing. It is this: *Let the body—not the hands—start moving the club on the downswing.*

Once you can do this you are on the road to vastly better golf. You will have the feeling that you are starting down with arms and club close to the body—close to the axis—where they should be at this time.

So much has been written over the years about the importance of the hands in swinging the club, that many of us are entirely too hand conscious. A standing vote of thanks is due Bill Casper for stating, in a description of his swing as it reached the hitting position: "At this point my body is still swinging the club." Many of us have been sure of that for years, but Casper, to our knowledge, was the first of the top tournament pros with the courage to say it.

The hands will take over soon enough, as an automatic, reflex action. The problem is to keep them out while still keeping them moving. If we keep them out while our body moves the club from the top, our timing will be far better.

Rhythm and Tempo

Rhythm and tempo can be considered together, because in golf they mean very nearly the same thing.

We mentioned earlier that the rhythm in the swing of a good player is noticed because of the measured cadence in the upward and downward movement of the club. In his swing there appears to be—and there is—a definite relationship in time between his backswing and his downswing. It is measured in two parts, from the time the club leaves the ball until it stops at the top of the backswing, and from the time it starts to move again until it hits the ball. The club does have to stop at the top, of course, for the instant required to reverse its direction, whether we feel it or realize it or we don't. No object, not even a golf club, can be traveling in opposite directions at once.

These two segments of the swing can be accurately timed by a motion-picture camera, by the simple process of counting the number of pictures the camera takes during each segment. Such a count shows that the backswing of a good player takes almost exactly twice as long as the downswing.

This two-to-one ratio is the rhythm of the swing. The total time or tempo of the swing will vary with different good players, but the ratio or rhythm will not. Nor will it vary from club to club. The ratio will be the same for the 8 iron as it is for the driver. The tempo of the swing will not change, either, for the individual player.

This is why the good player looks so good when he swings at the ball. There seems to be a definite, unhurried, relationship between the two parts of his swing. We sense it if we see him hit the ball only once, and it becomes more and more marked the oftener we see him swing. He has established a definite rhythm and he sticks to it. In fact, one of the things he does when he goes to the practice tee before a round is re-establish his rhythm, so that he hits a 5 iron, for instance, at exactly the same speed, with exactly the same effort, with exactly the same tempo, each time he swings it, whether the shot is simple or difficult.

We will always remember Jimmy Demaret playing the twelfth hole at Inverness in the National Open of 1957. Demaret was in contention and his drive on this hole wound up near the right edge of the fairway. It is a par 5 hole with the first half downhill, the second half uphill. Jimmy's drive had caught a slight downslope, so that he had a downhill lie. He was standing slightly above his ball. It was a most difficult shot to be made with a wooden club. To reach the green, Jimmy had to use the wood. His swing was as smooth and unhurried as if he had been hitting an 8 iron from a perfect lie to an open green. He hit it with his own established rhythm, and he reached the green with a perfect shot.

The poor or average player has no such established rhythm. Not only does he often have a different rhythm for each club but for different shots with the same club. He is prone to use a 7 and swing faster, when he should be using a 6 with a normal swing. He changes again to dig a ball out of the rough or a bad lie on the fairway. He slows down when he tries to steer the ball. He always speeds up when the situation of the round or match has increased his tension. Most of these changes are noticeable in his backswing, which becomes faster, sometimes almost as fast as his down-swing.

This is why his swing looks so bad and the pro's looks so good.

Why, you may ask, should anyone bother to develop a rhythmic swing? Aside from how it looks, of what value is it?

It has two very definite values. One is that it promotes better timing. It doesn't assure or guarantee that we will time a shot better, but it helps. It makes good timing easier to achieve.

The second reason is that a rhythmic swing helps a great deal toward the goal of every swing, which is to strike the ball in the exact center of the club face—"on the screws," as the pros say. There is a very small area on the face, known to all golfers as the "sweet spot," which transmits the maximum propelling force. When contact is made on this spot, the ball will go much farther than if the contact is toward the club's heel or toe.

Pertinent here are tests made for the United States Golf Association by the Arthur D. Little Co., a research organization, during the United States Amateur Championship at Brookline in 1957. Pictures were taken of the contact between club and ball. These were compared with the distance attained and with the velocity of the club head at impact.

Among the conclusions drawn by the USGA was that accuracy of contact was highly important in gaining distance. By accuracy was meant contact with the exact center of the club face. Distance dropped, even with a faster swing, if contact was not made precisely at the center.

The average golfer rarely gets this perfect, flush contact, although most of the time he isn't conscious of not getting it. He thinks of it only when he hits the ball well out toward the toe or in toward the heel, or toward the top or the sole. The pros, on the other hand, hit many shots on the sweet spot, and many more which are very close to it. This is one of the reasons they hit the ball as far as they do. And one of the reasons they find the sweet spot and get close to it so often, is because their swings are grooved in a constant, unhurried rhythm.

We are not saying that everyone should swing the club at exactly the same speed. Each of us has his own tempo of doing things, depending on his individual temperament. Some of us drive automobiles faster than others, eat faster, walk faster. We are likely to have faster golf swings. The point is that whatever speed we use to swing the club, it should always be the same, regardless of the lie we have, the difficulty of the shot, or the length of the shot. If we have to change our rhythm to get a longer shot with a 5 iron, we should use the 4 and keep the rhythm the same. The good pro knows that he will get 160 yards with a 5 iron, and he will get it every time, not 153 yards once, 165 yards the second time, and maybe 160 the next, assuming he hits the ball squarely each time. He will get it because his rhythm is constant.

So determine your own rhythm, with the help of your pro, and then stick to it, for all shots and with all clubs. It will make the game a lot easier.

In arriving at a proper speed for yourself, you should not swing so fast that you cannot feel or sense each of the fundamental moves that you make. These are the forward press, the immediate backward wrist break, the movement of the weight, the turn of the shoulders to the top, the lateral slide of the hips, and the slightly rocking action of the shoulders that start the downswing, and the definite feeling that the body is swinging the club until it gets near the ball. If, then, you can feel the hard forward swinging of the hands through the ball, so much the better.

We do not mean, we will hasten to say, that you should think of each of these movements each time you swing the club, or that you should feel each one separately every time you swing. What we do mean is that if at any time your pro should ask you what you feel you are doing at any stage of your swing, you can tell him, truthfully and exactly.

It is a fact, often brought out in lessons, that the average player has no idea what he feels or what he is doing during a large area of the swing. He will be conscious of starting the club away from the ball and getting it, maybe, halfway to the top. But from there on his mind is a blank. This is because emotion (in the form of fear of a bad shot) takes over and wipes all conscious thought from the mind. This "blacking out" is gradually overcome as the player gains confidence. His fear of a bad shot subsides to some extent, reason returns, and he has at least a partial feeling and memory of what he is doing.

For this reason it is important, in building a swing, to start it at a slow tempo, so that the player can feel all the movements. As these are executed correctly and become habit, the tempo may be increased.

We cannot tell anybody how hard to swing, because everyone has his own speed or tempo. We can only say that you should develop a definite rhythm, that you should swing with the same effort every time, and that this should not exceed the speed at which you know what you are doing all the time.

How the Early Break Helps

Strange as it may seem, the early backward wrist break is a positive aid to both timing and rhythm. Considering all the other good things the break does for us, this is icing on the cake. But it is true.

To understand precisely how this happens we will take another and closer look at the break itself, and also at the human wrist.

Let's take the wrist first. As any doctor will tell you, this is one of the most complex joints in the body. It is not a simple hinge like the elbow or the knee, nor a ball-and-socket joint like the hip. The wrist consists, in the main, of seven small bones and seven ligaments, and there are four basic directions in which it may move: (1) toward the palm of the hand (palmar flexion), (2) toward the back of the hand (dorsal flexion), (3) toward the little finger (ulnar deviation), and (4) toward the thumb (radial deviation). Any other movement represents a combination of the basics. The maximum unaided movement of the normal wrist is: palmar flexion, 90 degrees; dorsal flexion, 90 degrees; ulnar deviation, 45 degrees; radial deviation, 35 degrees.

The only motion that need concern us here is the last, for it is the radial deviation that the left wrist finally assumes

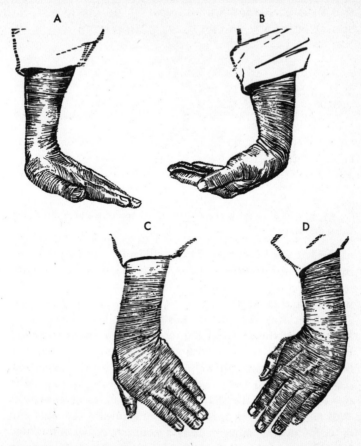

Figs. 50A, 50B, 50C, 50D. The basic movements of the hand at the wrist joint: A, dorsal flexion; B, palmar flexion; C, ulnar deviation; D, radial deviation.

at the top of the backswing *when it is in the proper position.*

Where 98 per cent of golfers go wrong is in getting this radial deviation *along with* a dorsal flexion at the top—the left hand bent backward and the left wrist under the shaft. This is the easy, the lazy, and the disastrous position. It leaves the club face open.

Now, you can get the correct position, with only a radial deviation, if you take the club back with rigid wrists and no break until the shaft is parallel with the line of flight or beyond it, and then break the wrists straight up, in the radial direction, being careful not to let any backward flexion

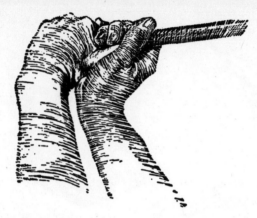

Fig. 51. The final position of the wrists at the top of the swing, showing radial deviation.

of the left wrist creep in. This is difficult, very difficult, and requires a great deal of practice to be done consistently, under all conditions, but it is worth noting that a lot of the pros do it that way.

Another way the correct position can be reached is by a rotation of the hands at the top or during the downswing. You can reach the top with the left hand in an extreme backward flex and the club face wide open, and then straighten out the left wrist. This pulls the right wrist under the shaft, rotates the shaft itself, and squares or closes the club face. Seen from the side, looking toward the butt end of the club, the movement is a counterclockwise rotation. When it is completed, the player has the true radial deviation he wants.

Far easier than either of these methods is the early backward break already taught in this book, which amounts to a palmar flex of the left wrist and a dorsal flex of the right. The great virtues of this are that it gets us as far away as possible from the lazy backward flex of the left wrist and that it flows or molds naturally as we bring the club up, into the pure radial deviation as we reach the top. Try it and see. Make the backswing at reduced speed and notice and feel how the wrist and hand position changes as the hands go up past the shoulders. By the time the swing reaches the top the left hand will have gone from a palmar flexion to a radial deviation without any effort on your part. It is the natural tendency. The only thing you have to watch is that it doesn't go too far and fall into a backward flex.

So why not use the break that brings you to the top naturally in the right position, instead of a break that you have to control carefully or manipulate?

Without going any further into anatomical details, it can be stated flatly that the longer the backward wrist break is delayed on the backswing, the more difficult it becomes to make it correctly. The later this break takes place, the more liable we are to let the left hand bend backward, thus getting it under the shaft at the top and opening the face of the club. So, make the break early.

Start making it as soon as the club leaves the ball and you will find it does a surprising number of things. We'll list them:

1. Sets you in the proper hand-wrist position early. (All you have to do is hold it.)
2. Everything you have to do with the hands and the club, in the way of manipulation, is done early and in your full view.
3. Gives you the feeling that you have plenty of time to go to the top and come down.
4. Starts your swing in the right plane.
5. Brings the right elbow in tight immediately.
6. Prevents a "bouncing" club head at the top.
7. Tends to shorten the swing, thereby providing a brace against overswinging.
8. Gives you a feeling at the top that you *have* to move the body in order to get the club down to the ball. (Reduces inclination to hit from the top.)
9. Tends to bring the club to the ball with the wrists leading, as they should be.
10. Kills any temptation to pronate or supinate.
11. Promotes—almost insures—a late hit.
12. Promotes a solid contact on the center of the club face.

The first three points are probably the most important. The others stem chiefly from the first three.

One of the hardest things for the average golfer to master is the proper hand and wrist position at the top. At least one reason this is difficult for him is that, with the orthodox late break, he is always trying to get into it after the swing is in full motion. The early break sets his hands in the proper positions by the time they are hip high.

Another value is that this break divorces your mind from the club head. In the orthodox late break, with what has been called the one-piece takeaway, the player is thinking of moving hips, hands, and club head all at the same time. The fact that he is thinking of the club head at all is dangerous. With the early break completed, there comes a feeling of time to spare. Nothing else needs to be done, except to swing the club to the top and bring it down. The hands will be right, the wrists will be right, the face of the club will be right—all you have to do is swing.

This feeling of what might almost be called serenity, plus points 4, 5, and 6, all contribute to getting you to the top of the swing in an excellent position. And the right position at the top goes a long, long way toward insuring a good downswing.

All Quiet at the Top

One reason that the early break seems almost to keep us from hitting too soon is that with it we reach the top with a controlled, "quiet" club head. With the ordinary wrist break, which is late, the club head moves quite fast in the late stages of the backswing. It moves fast enough, in fact, to exert a strong pull on the hands and wrists as it reaches its backward limit. Its momentum, actually, is checked only by the resistance of the hands and wrists to this pull. As a result, in answer to this resistance of the hands and wrists, there is a quick rebounding of the club back toward the ball. Try it and you'll see what we mean. Since the average player usually lets the backward pull loosen his grip, he quickly regrips on the rebound, producing, almost, a "bouncing" club head. This starts the head of the club back toward the ball much faster than it should be moving at this point. This is one reason, and a strictly mechanical reason, why so many of us hit from the top.

Now, with the early backward break you do not get this bouncing effect at the top. From the time the hands are hip high only the arms, actuated by the shoulders, are moving the club. The club itself is not moving fast as it reaches the limit of the backswing, and there is a noticeable but not violent pull on the hands and wrists when it gets there.

Hence there is no rebound. The club starts down solely in response to the shoulder and hip action—and we are off to a late hit (point No. 11) instead of an early one.

Since the late hit is the true manifestation of good timing, you have, right there, one reason the early backward break promotes good timing. The fact that there is no rebounding from the top, and no hurried effort then to get the club head to the ball, is also why this system makes it easier to establish a good, even rhythm.

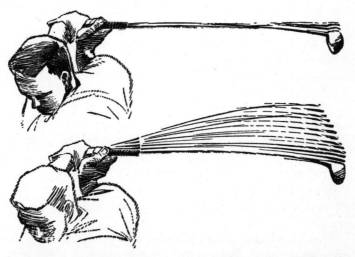

Fig. 52. The quiet club at the top of the swing (top) depends on the early backward wrist break. The bouncing club (bottom) originates in the conventional late break.

But, you will say, the pros have no trouble with the late break and this rebounding of the club head. No, they don't, because they subconsciously time their movements with it and also because they "tame" the club head by keeping a tight grip at the top. This grip is tight enough so that the club never gets away from them. But for the average player the timing is much more difficult.

Point 8, the feeling that you have to move the body to get the club down to the ball, has its origin in the fact that for the last half of the backswing you are moving the club largely with your body and shoulders. You are not moving it by breaking your wrists. So, since you have brought the club back with your body and shoulders, the natural thing to do is simply to leave them in command and start the downswing with them. This is exactly what should be done—the hips sliding laterally, and turning and rocking the shoulders to bring the club down.

Points 9 and 10—the wrists leading at impact with no temptation to pronate or supinate—are accounted for largely by the position the early break puts the hands and wrists into, aided by the fact that the body is swinging the club during a large segment of the downswing. With the perfect late hit, when the club catches up with the hands at the last possible moment, the hands will always be slightly in front at impact. The club has caught up enough to strike a straight, solid blow, but it doesn't get exactly even with the hands until slightly after the ball is hit. This will vary among the top pros, but pictures of many of them, taken at impact, show the left arm and the club in a curving line, not a straight line. Bill Casper and Wes Ellis are two examples.

The fact that a solid contact is produced on the center of the club face is, really, the cumulative effect of many of the movements which have preceded it. Whenever the hit is late and from the inside the contact is much more likely to be accurate than if we hit too soon and/or from the outside.

There is another minor phenomenon associated with the early-break system. Practically everyone to whom it has been taught will say, usually during his second or third lesson, what a business executive at the Rockaway River Country Club in New Jersey said: "I have a strong feeling that the club head is going through the ball faster and that I am swinging harder than I ever did before, but I am not trying to."

This, besides being a compliment to the teacher, is an indication that the system is working. The executive felt the club was going faster because it *was* going faster. The speed was greater because he was hitting later. And he felt he was swinging harder because of the speed he was getting in the club head.

Many also get the feeling that, as one of them put it, "All of me is going into the shot now." They get this because they are moving the club with their bodies as they bring it down and are not trying, with their hands, to make the club head move.

As a result of all this, the first pleasant surprise a pupil gets as he learns the system is greater distance. This will come with the pitching clubs first, because they are the shortest and easiest to handle. And it will come with all players, regardless of age, sex, strength, or physical build.

Which, of course, is perfectly natural and logical. When you hit the ball late and from the inside it will go farther than from any other kind of a hit. And if you hold the wrist position at the top and then move so that you come down behind the ball while your hips are out in front of it, you will hit from the inside and you will hit late. There is nothing else you can do. That is the crowning virtue of the system.

As a Rockaway River member who has been playing golf for forty-five years put it: "This I can feel as well as understand; all other instruction I have understood but not necessarily felt."

11 *Thinking Your Way Around*

So far, everything in this book has dealt with the physical actions of golf, the positions and movements of our hands, our feet, our bodies, our arms, and of the club itself. There is another side of golf, though, that is all too frequently overlooked in our sometimes frantic efforts to master the swing. This is the mental or thinking side of the game. Happily, this is not nearly so difficult to master as the rest.

Basically, the thinking side of the game is the exercise of common sense, by which we give ourselves the best possible chance on every shot we undertake, adapting ourselves to the elements of wind, weather, and terrain, using our clubs to their fullest capabilities. We plan how we are going to play each shot, how we are going to position ourselves and our ball to play each hole.

The more talented or expert a player is, the more likely he is to carry out his plans. He has the ability to make the ball do, most of the time, what he wants it to do, within varying limits. The poorer player does not have this fine control of the ball, and he does not hit it so far, but he should plan every shot and every hole. He will not be able to carry out his plans as often as the good player, but when he does, they will save him strokes, and obviously the poorer player should overlook no opportunity whatever to reduce his shots.

The playing of a round of golf is a long succession of decisions on what to do, followed by the physical action of carrying them out. The physical action may be good but may fall short of success if the decision is wrong. For instance, having hit a fine drive, you decide the 8 iron will carry the trap and put your ball on the green. You hit the iron perfectly—and drop the ball into the trap. The execution was faultless but the decision was wrong. You should have used your 7.

The selection of clubs, though, is only one area of the thinking department. A larger area is the planning of a shot to avoid trouble. This is, in a sense, a negative or defensive type of thinking, but it is extremely important. There are players who glory in playing everything boldly, in

San Diego Express Charters

Catch The Wave

Marv Atchley
Motorcoach Operator
P.O. Box 13159
San Diego, CA. 92170-3159
Phone: (619) 233-1292
Fax: (619) 696-5173
Email: sdxinc@aol.com
www.sdxcharters.com

nd in scorning caution in
when you stop to think of it,
ayer or the average player or
ave of beating the golf course?
ately well equipped individual,
x thousand yards of rolling coun-
atural and man-made hazards. For
t this enemy is asinine. The course
The only sane attitude for any ordi-
is the defensive one, charting his way
lurking dangers (thumbing his nose at
haps), but at all costs avoiding them.

in, the fatal flaw, if you will, in the poor
, is attempting too much. He gambles, on
of sheer hope, that he will make a great shot
osition when the odds are heavy that he would
arly as good a shot from a perfect position. He
takes a n when he knows he should take a 4, because the
others in the foursome are using 5's. He attempts to carry
a trap from the tee when he knows in his heart that only
a perfect shot, which he rarely hits, will get him over it.
He tries to get distance from the rough when all he should
try to do is just get out. In short, hope and pride—and
apparently a belief in miracles—cause the average player to
attempt too much. By trying to beat the course to its knees
when he should only be outboxing it, the typical player
loses strokes.

For the expert the situation is different. For him the bold
attack is fine, tempered with reasonable good sense. He has
the game that can beat the course, and he will beat it only
if he attacks it.

A perfect example of a top pro attacking a course was
Arnold Palmer on the first hole of the last round at Cherry
Hills in 1960. Palmer started that last round seven shots
behind the leader. He knew that only the boldest of play
could close the gap. The first hole was a par 4, slightly downhill, measured 346 yards, and the green was closely guarded
by traps, although there was a narrow opening. Palmer let
out the shaft, as the pros say, and drove the green. He got
down in two putts for a birdie 3, was off to a fast start, and
as it turned out, a victorious round. Palmer has the power-

ful game to beat any course. He kept attacking Cherry Hills, subdued it with a 65, and won the Open.

Before we go into the specifics of thinking, there are two things we can all do. We can learn both the rules and the etiquette of golf. The rules are many and they are sometimes peculiar, but the etiquette is simple. It is merely the application of the golden rule to golf: "Do unto others as you would have them do unto you."

Most of the rules of golf are restrictive; they tell us what we cannot do. But many of them afford us relief, too, from particular situations. Be certain you know the rules on a lost ball, out of bounds, an unplayable lie. Learn the rules governing water hazards and lateral water hazards. Know what a hazard itself is and what you are permitted and not permitted to do when your ball is in one. Familiarize yourself with the rules on obstructions, and bear in mind always that you cannot "move, bend, or break anything fixed or growing" except in special circumstances. Read, also, the rules on casual water, on obstructions deriving from course maintenance, and read the local rules printed on the scorecard. Sometimes you find some surprises in the latter.

The rules and etiquette are issued annually in booklet form by the United States Golf Association, the best and wisest sports governing body in America. You owe it to yourself to have a copy.

The Weapons We Use

Since we play this game with clubs, our first thinking should be about the weapons we use. And there is plenty of material for thought here. How heavy should they be, what should be their swing weight, how stiff should the shafts be, how many should we carry, and which ones should they be?

Weights of clubs seem to go in cycles. In the early 1930's the tournament pros felt that with light clubs they could swing faster and thereby get more distance. The word spread about how the pros felt, the demand for light clubs increased, and the manufacturers of course obliged. This lasted until somewhere in the 1940's, when the pros decided that with heavier clubs they expended less physical effort; they would, in effect, let the club do the work. So heavier clubs came in. By 1960 the trend had begun to go the other way, toward slightly lighter sticks, not much but a little.

We prefer a club a little on the heavy side, for the reason that it doesn't have to be swung so fast. It can, and will, do most of the work if it is given a chance. With such a club the player can concentrate more on swinging correctly, making the proper moves that will bring direction, and not concern himself with getting adequate distance.

The average driver today weighs 13¼ to 13½ ounces and is 43 inches long, measured from the base of the heel to the tip of the shaft. The other woods are shorter by about a half inch with each number. The No. 2 iron is about 38½ to 38⅝ inches, and the others drop about ⁷⁄₁₆ of an inch each, down to the No. 9. The irons weigh from 14½ ounces for the No. 2 to 16½ for the No. 9. Sand wedges will go up to 17½.

Shafts of clubs are graded in three types, flexible, medium, and stiff. Most of the bigger, stronger pros use the stiff shaft. The medium shaft is for the average player. The flexible is generally considered best for players of more advanced age and for women. It is best suited for a slow swing. The limberness of a shaft is known to the manufacturers as *shaft deflection*.

The amount of loft in the face of a club (the amount it inclines from the vertical) varies from 10½ degrees for the driver up to 58 degrees for the sand wedge. There is only one degree difference between the No. 4 wood (19 degrees) and the No. 2 iron (20 degrees). Here are the lofts of the standard clubs:

Woods		Irons	
Driver	10½ degrees	No. 2	20 degrees
No. 2	13 degrees	No. 3	23 degrees
No. 3	16 degrees	No. 4	27 degrees
No. 4	19 degrees	No. 5	31 degrees
No. 5	21 degrees	No. 6	35 degrees
		No. 7	39 degrees
		No. 8	43 degrees
		No. 9	47 degrees
		Pitching wedge	53 degrees
		Wedge	55 degrees
		Sand wedge	58 degrees

We have heard a great deal, for years, about swing weight. The term is tossed about so loosely, in fact, that few players have much of an idea what it is. Swing weight indicates the distribution of the weight of a club. It is the proportion of the weight in the head compared to the shaft and the grip. Swing weights are listed from C—0 to D—9.

But a D—9, for instance, doesn't mean that 9 ounces of club weighing 13¼ ounces are in the head. D—9 is merely one of the calibrations on what is known as a *lorythmic* swinging weight scale.

A D—9 is no club for the average player to use, either. It is what Arnold Palmer and many of the other pros use, and it is for a strong, fast swinger. For the average player the ideal swing weight is from D—1 to D—4. For women the range is from C—4 to C—6.

In a general sense, the more you "feel" the head of the club when you waggle it or swing it, the higher the swing weight. You have often heard players say, and no doubt you have said it yourself, when handling a new club, "Feels like a lot of head in this." What you are feeling is the swing weight.

You could be fooled, of course, by the shaft. A medium swing weight, for instance, in a club with a flexible shaft, would feel like a very high swing weight. You would "feel" an inordinate amount of head when you swung it. In fact, with a club like this, you would have a very difficult time developing a decent swing at all. But the manufacturers have taken care of this. They do not put out clubs with high swing weights on flexible shafts. In men's clubs the swing weights for a flexible shaft are D—0 and D—1. For medium shafts they are D—1 to D—4. For stiff shafts they are D—4 to D—9.

Which Clubs to Carry

Since the USGA permits the carrying of fourteen clubs, it would be difficult to persuade the average golfer that he shouldn't take full advantage of the rule. He would not be happy, indeed he would feel himself laboring under a handicap, carrying fewer than the rule allows. So, which ones should they be?

From the conventional set of three woods, nine irons, a sand wedge, and a putter, the average player should drop the No. 1 iron and the No. 2 wood. For these he should substitute the No. 4 wood and a pitching wedge. The No. 2 wood and the No. 1 iron, with their relatively straight faces, are the hardest clubs of all to use. Many pros dispense with the No. 2 wood, the old brassie, though most of them carry a No. 1 iron, mostly for use off a tee. If the pros cannot use them effectively, what chance does a 16-handicapper have to make them behave?

It is also a fact that most golfers find a lofted wood easier to handle than a long iron. This seems to be specially true as the player grows older. If you are one of these, and do not want to or cannot take the time to master the longer irons, then drop out the No. 2 and pick up a No. 5 wood.

Generally speaking, we recommend the carrying of a driver, Nos. 3 and 4 woods, Nos. 2, 3, 4, 5, 6, 7, 8, and 9 irons, a pitching wedge, a sand wedge, and a putter.

There are some to whom the No. 1 wood, the driver, seems to be a special type of poison. There is no logical reason for this. Anybody who can hit a 3 wood, or any other wood, off the fairway has more than enough ability to hit a teed-up ball with a driver. If you hook or slice so badly with the driver that you are afraid to play it, something is radically wrong with your swing.

Strategy on the Tee

Now that we have decided on our clubs, let us go to the first tee. You have the option of teeing your ball anywhere between, but not forward of, the markers. Don't forget that you can also tee it a maximum of two club-lengths behind the line of the markers.

Before you stick the peg in the ground take a good look at what is in front of you. And know what you are looking for. Almost every hole has more trouble on one side of the fairway than it does on the other. This trouble may be obvious: a string of white out-of-bounds stakes, a fence, or a pond. It may be more subtle: longer rough on one side than on the other, or a fairway trap on one side. It might be just a line of small trees, or a hidden ravine, or it might be one big tree with spreading branches out there in the rough about 220 or 230 yards from the tee.

Whatever the trouble is, make this your rule: Tee up your

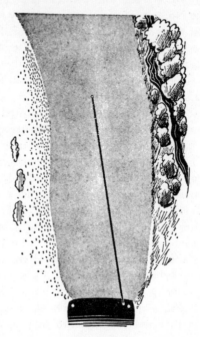

Fig. 53. Faced with rough, trees, and a brook at the right of the fairway and only mild rough at the left, tee the ball on the right side and shoot away from the trouble.

ball on the same side of the teeing ground as the trouble lies, and shoot away from it.

If the worst trouble lies on the right side, tee up on the right. Aim for the left center of the fairway and let fly. This way you will be at least starting your shot away from the danger zone. If, playing from the right side, you slice badly enough to bring the ball back into the trouble, you will still have two sources of satisfaction: The ball won't be as deep in the trouble and you will know that you at least tried intelligently to avoid it. There is always the chance, of course, that you will hit the ball across the fairway and into the rough on the opposite side, but then you have been caught by the lesser of the two evils and the advantage is still yours.

Something else in teeing your ball. Take advantage, if there is any to be taken, of any unevenness of the ground. Often there are little depressions on a tee. If there are in the area you choose, tee your ball on the forward edge of one. This will give you a slightly uphill lie, the lie most golfers like to play from. This is especially important if you are playing with the wind behind you. It will get your ball a little higher. But wherever you tee, be sure there are no obstructions of any kind behind the ball. These might be worm casts, which could deflect the club slightly as it is brought back, or they could be loose, dead grass, the movement of which might distract you. Whatever they are, get rid of them.

Another point to be sure of is that your feet are on level ground, that there is nothing under them which disturbs you, like a stick or a small stone or a clod of mud. Be sure also, especially in wet weather, that your feet aren't resting on muddy ground or loose earth from which they might slip.

All this may seem to be making mountains out of those worm casts we warned you of, but such observation, inspection, and reaction should become automatic. We assure you they are with the good player. Any little advantages which may exist are even more valuable to you than they are to the pro or the low-handicap player.

Handling the Wind

One of the great and variable hazards of golf is the wind. Few players actually like the wind, because it is an unsettling factor, though sometimes more imaginary than real. It is a fact, though, that an appreciable number of yards are lost when you hit straight into a wind, even though it is a light breeze, and just as many yards are gained when the wind is directly with the shot.

It follows, then, that in playing against the wind the ball should be kept as low as possible, where it is less exposed, and that when the wind is behind us we should get the ball up so the movement of air can exert a greater and longer effect. To get a low ball, play it back farther than normal, toward the center line between the feet if it is the tee shot, back farther for a pitching iron. Keep more weight on the left leg than normally and try to have your hands ahead of the ball at impact. It is also advisable, against the wind, to take one club stronger than you would use in still air, grip it shorter, and use a shorter but firmer swing. Most of these alterations should be reversed in a following wind. The ball should be played a shade farther forward than usual to get it up quickly, and one club weaker than normal should be used. It, too, should be gripped shorter and swung with a shorter and firmer action. Let the weight movement and the hand action be normal; fooling with them is too dangerous.

Playing in a crosswind from the tee, the ball should be played from the same side the wind is blowing and played for the windward side of the fairway. This way you are letting the wind help the ball just a little, instead of fighting it as you would be if you started the ball even slightly against it. This formula—playing from the side of the tee the wind is blowing from—holds in a quartering wind too, whether it is with or against you.

You will be faced with a slight conflict if the trouble is on one side of the fairway and the wind is coming from the other. When you find yourself in this dilemma, let the trouble be the determining factor.

One more thought while we are on the teeing ground. Most short (par 3) holes are played with an iron. When you play them, use a wooden tee. This is the only chance you ever have to get a perfect lie for an iron, so why not take it? But remember, the higher you tee the ball, the less distance you will get.

You can make this knowledge work for you. For instance, you may come to a hole which is a little short for the 5 iron you feel you should use but not short enough for a 6. Your feeling is that if you use the No. 6 you will have to hit the ball very hard to get there. In this case use the 5 but tee your ball a little higher and use your normal swing. The higher tee will take distance off the shot. You can vary the height of the tee in the wind, too, teeing a shade higher if you want the help of a following wind and lower if you want a low, boring shot into the wind.

Have an Eye for Position

Another area in which you can use your heads is getting position for a shot to the green. This consists merely of trying to get your ball in front of the opening to the green, whether that opening is 10 yards away or 180.

On a short or medium-length par-4 hole, try to place your drive so that you can aim your second shot at the opening and not have to approach the green from an angle where there is no opening and you will have to carry a trap to reach the putting surface. If the opening, let's say, on a 330-yard hole is at the left, aim your tee shot down the left side of the fairway. Then you can aim for the green over the opening and, if your shot is straight but somewhat short, you will still be in good position, with a good lie from which to chip up and get your par anyway. If your drive is down the right side, though, you probably will have to go over a trap to reach the green. If you mis-hit the shot you will be in the trap, and if you hit it too hard or use a stronger club to be sure you carry the trap, you may go over the green or wind up high on the rear of it from where you may easily take three putts. On par-5 holes your second shot is the one to place with an eye to the opening. Where the opening is no problem, shoot for the big or deep part of the green, the so-called "fat" of it. These are small things, of course, but in the course of eighteen holes they can save you a surprising number of shots.

For the average player the wood or the long iron from the fairway is the hardest shot in the game. His big trouble is getting the ball up in the air, unless the ball is sitting up high, begging to be hit—a situation that doesn't often occur.

Obviously this shot has to be struck accurately or, with a straight-faced club, the ball won't get up. But what complicates the problem is that distance also is needed. So the average player swings hard to get that distance. The harder he swings, the less chance he has to strike the ball accurately. He half tops it or he hits behind it, and the shot is missed.

If this shot is giving you trouble, the first thing to remember is to select a club with enough loft; not the No. 2 wood, maybe not even the No. 3. The next thing to recall is that the longer the club, the harder it is to control. So shorten your grip on the No. 3, say, perhaps halfway down the gripping area. This shortens the club. And then don't try to kill the ball. Use a controlled swing, a little shorter than normal, and try only for a perfect contact. It will help, too, to address the ball with your hands just a shade in front of it, as you might for a short iron, so that the arc of the swing is slightly downward through the ball. For remember, it is hitting down on a ball that gets it up. Remember, likewise, that distance comes as much from a square, flush contact as from club head speed.

In playing any wood shot from the fairway, take a good look at your lie before you pull a club from the bag. If

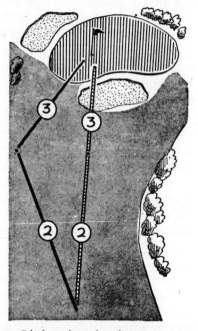

Fig. 54. On a par-5 hole such as this, the correct route for the second and third shots is the solid black line to the left. The same route would hold if this were a par 4 and the approach shot were the second instead of the third. An approach through an opening to a deeper part of a green is always less dangerous.

it is in the least downhill use a No. 4 wood, perhaps even a No. 5. Your chance of making a good shot will be much better.

When the Track Is Wet

Wet weather is another hazard. The first move to make when the rain is coming down and the course is soggy, is to resign yourself to it. You are not going to hit the ball as far as you usually do and you are not going to score as well. But there are things you can do. Use your umbrella to the best advantage and keep as dry as possible. Have your caddy hold it over you while you thoroughly size up the shot. Then step out, hit the shot—but don't hurry it—and then get back under. Be sure your caddy carries an extra towel to wipe off the clubs. Be careful, in your waggle, that the club doesn't pick up cut grass on its face. The crushing of the grass between ball and club face makes for a slippery contact; the ball may duck, squirt off, or do other peculiar things. You will find at times that it is impossible to waggle at all, because of this pickup of grass. You must school yourself to be able to make shots without this usual preliminary. The cut grass can be especially troublesome just off the greens.

In playing an iron from wet turf keep in mind that an accurate contact is of prime importance. Shorten your grip a little, shorten the swing a little, keep more weight on the left foot than you normally do, and try to pick the ball off cleanly instead of going down and through it. Admittedly, this is somewhat dangerous. But the reasoning is clear: We want to avoid a contact that is in the least heavy. On dry turf you can often get away with a shot when you catch the ball a little heavy, because the iron will "ride" just a little on the grass. But in wet weather it won't. The sharp edge of the iron will dig into soft turf if you give it any chance at all. So a descending blow, which would take a divot, must be very accurate. If it hits even a shade behind the ball the shot is ruined. So in wet weather stay down to the ball and pick it off.

The rough always is tougher to get the club through when it is wet, so take extra pains to avoid it. When you do get in it, though, be sure you use a club with plenty of loft to get out, and take a slightly more upright swing.

No shot will run as far on wet turf as on dry, so on tee shots tee the ball a little higher to get as much carry as possible. A No. 2 wood from the tee, in fact, is not a bad club to use on a wet track.

In general, the average golfer should use the 4 wood

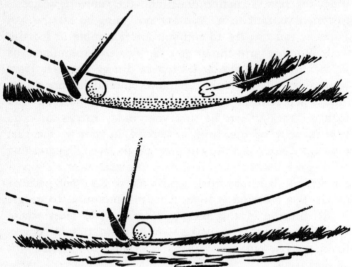

Fig. 55. Above, the normal iron shot in dry weather, taking the usual divot. Below, the pick-off type of shot to be played in wet weather or on a heavy course, the ball being taken clean.

on a wet fairway, rather than the 3. To reach a specific target he should use a club one number stronger than he would in dry weather, shorten his swing somewhat, and concentrate on meeting the ball squarely and getting it into the air. He can also play his approaches a little bolder up to the hole, knowing the ball will stick, and from around the fringe of the green he should use a more lofted club, pitching the ball a little more, rather than trying to run it on wet greens. In bunkers the sand will be heavier. Try for a slightly more shallow path through the sand for the club head; you can hit the same distance behind the ball as you would normally, but don't let the club dig quite so deep.

Since the greens will be slower, the putting can be bolder. Many players putt better on wet greens. A word of caution here: Be sure you get the short putts up to the hole. It's easy to leave the short ones short on a slow green.

As a final reminder for wet-weather play, be sure you know the rule on casual water, which is "any temporary accumulation of water which is visible before or after the player takes his stance." The key words here are "visible" and "before or after." If you can see the water, it is casual water and you are entitled to relief. This applies, on the green, not only to water between your ball and the cup but also to where you are taking your stance to hit the putt. It is also a fact that you may not be able to see any accumulation of water in the stance area as you are lining up your putt, but that it becomes visible after you have taken your stance —usually because the weight of your body forces it up through the turf.

Through the fairway or in the rough, of course, the rule applies only to the spot where the ball lies and where you stand to hit it, not to any puddles on the fairway 60 yards or so in front of you. And of course you do not have to play bunker shots out of water. You are permitted a free drop somewhere else in the bunker, though not nearer the hole. If the bunker is completely inundated you drop outside it.

But look up the rule, learn it, and use the relief it affords you. We have seen too many people try to putt through big puddles on greens without realizing they didn't have to.

The Payoff Area

Another area where there is plenty of room for headwork, of course, is on the greens and around them.

The prime object from close range is to get the ball as near the hole as possible. Ninety-nine times out of a hundred, though, there is still another shot to be made before you get the ball into the cup. It is this next one that you should have in the back of your head when you play the first one— the idea of making that next one as easy as you can.

The only things which can make the next one difficult, assuming it's a short pitch or a chip and that you get the ball three feet from the cup, are leaving the first one above the hole or to the side with a nasty roll. We all know that we approach a putt that is slightly uphill with much more confidence than one which is downhill or sidehill. So in sizing up the shot to a green where there are definite rolls near the cup, try to play it so that you reduce the odds against holing your next one. It's better to be left with a four-footer uphill than with a three-footer downhill or side-hill.

This also holds true for long approach putts, and with these you should be more successful in getting the ball where you want it, because most of us have more control with a putter than when we are chipping or hitting a short pitch.

Something to remember about rolls on a green is the distance of the roll from your ball. If it is near the ball it will have much less effect than if it is far away. This, of course, is because the ball will be moving faster right after you hit it than it will be as it nears the cup. A big roll near the ball will deflect it much less than a small roll near the cup. The knowledge of how much you should allow for each can only be gained by experience, and lots of it.

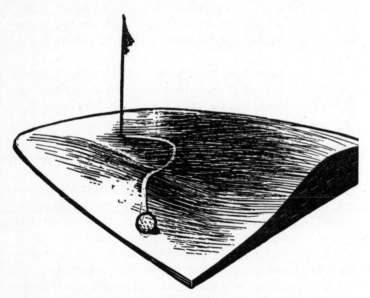

Fig. 56. Remember that a big side roll near the ball will not affect the path of a putt nearly as much as a small roll near the cup, when the ball has slowed down.

Grain is another thing to be taken into consideration. On putts with the grain of the grass, your ball will roll farther than it normally would. Against the grain, it won't roll as far. In putting across the grain the ball will be deflected in the direction toward which the grass points, and on a putt of any length you will have to allow for it. And grain varies widely. Some greens are very grainy, others only slightly so. Patches of some greens will be grainy, other areas won't be. So take a good look, especially around the cup. Again, experience will be your only guide.

When in doubt, and when it is possible without delaying play (and it usually is), look at your putt from the side as well as from behind the ball. You will get a better idea from the side whether your putt is slightly uphill or slightly downhill, and this knowledge can be invaluable in determining how hard to stroke the ball.

So far as boldness and caution are concerned the average player, as we have already noted, will be far better off playing safe than he will be by taking chances. This is especially true in medal play, where every stroke goes down on the card. The only time to take chances in a medal round is in the late stages when only bold play can give you a chance to win, or to qualify, or to reach whatever goal you have set.

Match play is a little different. Individual temperament is a factor here. Some players delight in match play and are at their best when engaged in it, knowing that no matter how many extra shots they take on a hole the price can only be the loss of that hole.

Still, in the long run, a reasonably safe type of operation will pay off in match play. As great a golfer as Bob Jones, who didn't like match play, played the card and let the match take care of itself. The best time to take chances in match play is when you are behind and the holes are running out. If you fall behind your opponent early in a match, one of the worst things you can do is panic and start going for everything. Usually you will only make it easier for him. In this situation it is far better to play the card and let your foe come back to you. It is amazing how often he will do just that.

Another thing about match play. Don't be liberal in conceding putts, unless you want to do it early in a round to build up a false sense of security in your opponent, which you will shatter in the late stages by making him hole out those little ones. It is always well to remember, though, that a putt that is short enough to be conceded is also short enough to be holed without difficulty. Your opponent has no right to take umbrage at being made to hole a putt he thinks you should give him. On your own part, it is well to get in the habit of never expecting any of your putts to be conceded. Then you never will be surprised when one isn't.

List Your Faults

As a general thought, every golfer should analyze his own game in two principal lights—his weaknesses in what might be called departmental areas, and the swing faults to which he is most prone.

A player may be an excellent driver but throw away strokes around the green. He may be an excellent chipper and putter but be wild off the tee. Some players are very good with the irons but woefully inept with the woods. These departmental strengths and weaknesses he knows well. If he is smart he will work on the shaky shots and at least try to bring them up to the rest of his game. The short game is easy to practice and develop. The long game is more of a problem, but if the basic principles are followed and continually checked, great strides can be made.

The swing faults are a little different, and too many players pay too little attention to them. For instance, one of the commonest faults you can slip into is cutting down on your shoulder turn, which usually causes your shots to stray off to the right. Another fault is moving your left hand up on top of the shaft in your grip. A third is unconsciously playing the ball farther back to a point midway between the feet or even farther. A fourth is letting your hands lag on the downswing. Still another might be working into a swing plane that is too upright. These are just samples. There are many others.

Our point is that each individual tends to develop certain faults and he develops them habitually, maybe two or three or four of them. One good player we know, who has played in the National Amateur championship several times, has a habit of addressing the ball for his drive farther and farther back toward the middle position. If he doesn't watch himself, he will have the ball back nearer his right foot than his left. This is something he has to check every so often.

If you have played much golf you are bound to have a pretty good idea of the bad habits you fall into in the course of a season. So sit down some night and analyze your game in the light of your swing faults. They are easy faults to forget. Make a list of them. Then check over the list before you next go out to play. One good place to put such a list is in your locker at the club. You can take a quick look at it, as a reminder, while you are dressing. Be on your guard against them as you walk to the first tee. If you begin to hit some bad shots you can immediately trace the shot to the fault and correct it.

One final thought, and this applies to all types of play, whether in competition, just for fun, or even if you are playing alone: *Never give up*. Golf is one of the most peculiar of all forms of contest. Form can be fleeting. Luck can change. Touch comes and goes. No matter how bad a start you may get on a round, keep trying. You never can tell when the bogeys and double bogeys you pile up on the first half-dozen holes or the first nine, can suddenly turn to pars and birdies on the back nine. It never pays to give up on yourself.

With this, we have covered the main areas in which our brains can be applied to this game. If we use them, from the time we step on the first tee until the last putt is holed, they will save us strokes. The more we save, the better scores we will have and the more pleasure and genuine satisfaction we will get from the game. If we don't think—if, as you have heard good players lament after a bad round, "I went to sleep out there"—we throw strokes away needlessly. Don't go to sleep. Plan and think on every shot. The ability to do this is the real meaning of concentration in golf.

ACKNOWLEDGMENTS

Many people have helped us in assembling material for this book or have helped in other aspects of its production. To all of them we are happy to express our gratitude.

Foremost on our list is Dr. Ira M. Freeman, professor of physics at Rutgers University. It was to him we went to learn the mechanical principle governing the action of the club in the last quarter of the downswing. His answer, the Conservation of Angular Momentum, cleared up one of the most puzzling aspects of the swing and became part of the foundation of this book.

Much of Dr. Freeman's conclusion was based on his study of multiflash photographs made by Dr. Harold E. Edgerton of Massachusetts Institute of Technology. To Dr. Edgerton we are indebted for the use of two of his photographs in this book, and for his sympathetic attitude toward our problem.

Our thanks also go to Jack Johnston, a *Newark News* photographer. He took several of the photographs we reproduce, and from hundreds more which he made (as well as several taken by Edward Dubin, a Rockaway River Country Club member), artist William Canfield made his drawings. Incidentally, all the drawings showing action were made from action photographs. There is no posed "action" in the book.

We thank golf professional Wesley Ellis for permitting us to use a photograph of his swing and for his appearance in certain of William Canfield's drawings.

Jimmy Demaret's remarks about the closed face and the early wrist break appeared in *Golf Magazine,* February, 1961, and for their inclusion we are indebted to Charles Price of that magazine.

Finally, our thanks go to A. G. Spalding & Brothers for technical information about club manufacture; to Dr. Lewis W. Brown for guidance on human anatomy; to T. Desmond Sullivan, former president of the Golf Writers Association of America; to Geoffrey Cousins, honorable secretary of the Association of Golf Writers, Great Britain; to Earl H. Tiffany, Jr., for the photograph of the bad hitting position; to Al Beissert, art director of the *Newark News,* and Dr. Glennis B. Rickert for their many favors.

Index

ABOUT THE AUTHORS

JOE DANTE is one of America's best-known teaching professionals. Like his father, the late James J. Dante, co-author of *The Nine Bad Shots of Golf*, Joe has concentrated on the teaching side of the game. The hours he spends each season on the tee and giving playing lessons will match those of any club pro in America. The esteem in which his club members hold him is attested to by the annual "day" given him—known as "Dante's Inferno." He has been so plied with gifts at these affairs that, on occasion, he has had to hire a truck to take them home. Dante is married and is the father of two boys. He was recently elected president of the New Jersey Professional Golfers' Association.

LEN ELLIOTT, sports editor of the *Newark News* since 1939, has studied and written extensively about both the technique and mechanics of the golf swing. As a senior golfer he has been a serious contender in both the New Jersey and New York Metropolitan championships, and in three attempts has thrice qualified sectionally in the USGA national senior championship. With Joe Dante he wrote *Stop That Slice;* with Jim Dante and Leo Diegel *The Nine Bad Shots of Golf.*